PRAISE FOR *BIGGER, FASTER LEADERSHIP*

I've led many organizations and each time it hit a ceiling it was either a people or process issue. In *Bigger, Faster Leadership* my friend Sam Chand helps us understand that your organizations' size and speed are controlled by its systems and structure. This book provides pragmatic ways of thinking and challenges us to make the necessary changes.

—JOHN C. MAXWELL, *NEW YORK TIMES* BESTSELLING AUTHOR AND SPEAKER

Sam Chand's teaching is a secret weapon resulting in the increase of effective materialization of your unrealized potential.

—BISHOP T. D. JAKES, *NEW YORK TIMES* BESTSELLING AUTHOR

Chand's unique insight and experience ensure that whatever proceeds from his hand and heart will encourage, equip, and inspire. *Bigger, Faster Leadership* shares valuable insights and a fresh perspective to the leader who is searching for that "something more" needed to unlock new levels of growth and progress.

—BRIAN HOUSTON, GLOBAL SENIOR PASTOR, HILLSONG CHURCH

Dr. Sam Chand unveils the behind the scenes organizational principles that lead to public successes. *Bigger, Faster Leadership* offers practical and easy to understand advice to create the systems and structures that will help your organization grow bigger faster.

—CRAIG GROESCHEL, PASTOR OF LIFE.CHURCH AND
NEW YORK TIMES BESTSELLING AUTHOR

Bigger, Faster Leadership shows us how to facilitate maximum growth without compromising compassion, conviction, and connection to those we serve. With timeless wisdom and cutting-edge relevancy, this book inspires us to maximize the impact we can have as leaders.

—CHRIS HODGES, SENIOR PASTOR, CHURCH OF THE HIGHLANDS;
AUTHOR OF *FRESH AIR* AND *THE DANIEL DILEMMA*

Sam Chand realizes that unless you ask questions, you don't get answers. In this book, we benefit hugely from his inquisitions, which ultimately incite new ideas and possibilities within us!

—BISHOP DALE CARNEGIE BRONNER, SR., D.MIN., AUTHOR AND FOUNDER,
SENIOR PASTOR OF WORD OF FAITH CATHEDRAL, ATLANTA, GEORGIA

Every time our church has needed adjustments in our structure, Sam has been instrumental and insightful in providing the right changes for us. Reading this book will give you the strength and courage to do what you know you need to do as a leader.

—Judah and Chelsea Smith, lead pastors of the City Church

Sam Chand is an extraordinary leader. In this book he uses his insight and years of experience to show that the greatest growth comes from the smallest of details. This book is a must-read for leaders!

—John and Lisa Bevere, founders of Messenger International and bestselling authors

Bigger, Faster Leadership will help you create systems and structures that will get you where you want to go. Sam Chand provides solutions that will work for you, your teams, and your organization.

—Jentezen Franklin, senior pastor, Free Chapel; *New York Times* bestselling author

Sam Chand will expand your thinking, give you fresh tools, and help you navigate your leadership journey. I highly recommend this book to you and your teams.

—Mark Batterson, *New York Times* bestselling author of *The Circle Maker*, lead pastor of National Community Church

This book will definitely assist every leader in getting to where they want to be faster and with greater accuracy. Thanks Sam for such a great book—it will help so many people.

—Phil Pringle, founder and president of C3 Church International

Sam has done it again—every paragraph in this book is loaded with pure leadership gold! This is a must-read for every leader and team member who dares to believe their company or church's best days are ahead!

—Jeff and Beth Jones, pastor, author, teacher, Valley Family Church and *The Basics with Beth*

This is definitely a book that we will use as a team for advancing and growing our church to the next level.

—Pastor Andre Olivier, senior pastor, Rivers Church South Africa; author of *Biblical Principles for Business Success* and *Finding a Way to Win*

Dr. Chand is a source of rare leadership wisdom that will expand your thinking. If you want to do something small or slow, then do not read this book!

—WILLIAM VANDERBLOEMEN, FOUNDER AND CEO,
VANDERBLOEMEN SEARCH GROUP

Bigger, Faster Leadership unlocks great hope for any leader who feels there is a gap between the vision and their reality. I highly recommend it to you.

—PAUL DE JONG, SENIOR PASTOR, LIFE CHURCH, NEW ZEALAND

Sam's fascinating case study of the building of the Panama Canal will challenge every leader to reassess their situation through fresh eyes. Best of all, it will encourage you not to quit.

—CAREY NIEUWHOF, AUTHOR AND FOUNDING PASTOR, CONNEXUS CHURCH

Everything about this book appeals to me. If you know Sam, this is his next great achievement. And if you don't know Sam, this book is an amazing place to start.

—PHIL COOKE, PH.D., FILMMAKER, MEDIA CONSULTANT, AND AUTHOR OF
UNIQUE: TELLING YOUR STORY IN THE AGE OF BRANDS AND SOCIAL MEDIA

Whether you lead a business, church, nonprofit, academic, or athletic organization, this book is a must!

—BRIAN DODD, CONTENT CURATOR FOR THE WEBSITE
BRIAN DODD ON LEADERSHIP; AUTHOR OF *10 INDISPENSABLE
PRACTICES OF THE 2-MINUTE LEADER*

Sam Chand shares valuable insight in this helpful book designed to give you practical tools for your own leadership journey, as well as driving organizational effectiveness.

—BRAD LOMENICK, FOUNDER, BLINC; AUTHOR, *H3
LEADERSHIP* AND *THE CATALYST LEADER*

This book is unique and innovative, and it contains remarkable, tangible examples of setbacks and solutions. *Bigger, Faster Leadership* will make you better in both leadership and life.

—DAVE MARTIN, FOUNDER OF ULTIMATE LIFE SEMINARS,
AUTHOR OF *12 TRAITS OF THE GREATS*

This book is a must-read for those who have lost the wind in their sails and need help in moving a big ship forward.

—MAURY DAVIS, SENIOR PASTOR, CORNERSTONE, NASHVILLE, TENNESSEE

Have you ever found yourself bursting with vision and goals, yet floundering on the pathway to arrive there? Dr. Chand is both the vision clarifier and vision actualizer. He equips us to realize our fullest potential.

—BENNY AND WENDY PEREZ, LEAD PASTORS, CHURCH LV

Sam doesn't discount good systems and strategies, but he helps us move beyond where they begin to stagnate the organization.

—RON EDMONDSON, PASTOR, AUTHOR, BLOGGER

Dr. Sam Chand is one of the most brilliant thought-leaders I know.

—DR. MARK J. CHIRONNA, CHURCH ON THE LIVING EDGE,
MARK CHIRONNA MINISTRIES, THE ISSACHAR INITIATIVE

God has used Sam often in my life to help me grow bigger and faster as a leader so I could lead bigger and faster growing ministries. Every leader should read this book!

—SHAWN LOVEJOY, FOUNDER AND CEO, COURAGETOLEAD.COM; AUTHOR,
BE MEAN ABOUT THE VISION: RELENTLESSLY PROTECTING WHAT MATTERS

I don't know of anyone more capable of addressing leadership and organizational structures than Dr. Sam Chand. I am so thrilled that he is making his thoughts available in this book. If you're going to go big, you better get it fast!

—MICHAEL PITTS, CORNERSTONE CHURCH, TOLEDO, OHIO

Bigger, Faster Leadership is a must-read for all who are trying to figure out the angst of leading.

—MIKE ROBERTSON, LEAD PASTOR, VISALIA FIRST ASSEMBLY

Very few can pinpoint the critical needs of an organization with high-level precision like Dr. Samuel Chand. Once again Dr. Chand unpacks a jewel.

—JEFF SCOTT SMITH, PRESIDENT, JSS CONSULTING INC.

If you need help focusing a vision, developing a plan, or building scalable systems, this is a great resource.

—MICHAEL LUKASZEWSKI, CEO, CHURCH FUEL

BIGGER
FASTER
LEADERSHIP

BIGGER
FASTER
LEADERSHIP

Lessons from the Builders of the Panama Canal

Samuel R. Chand

THOMAS NELSON
Since 1798

Published in Nashville, Tennessee, by Thomas Nelson. Thomas Nelson is a registered trademark of HarperCollins Christian Publishing, Inc.

Thomas Nelson titles may be purchased in bulk for educational, business, fund-raising, or sales promotional use. For information, please e-mail SpecialMarkets@ ThomasNelson.com

All Scripture quotations are from the Holy Bible, New International Version®, NIV®. Copyright © 1973, 1978, 1984, 2011 by Biblica, Inc.® Used by permission of Zondervan. All rights reserved worldwide. www.zondervan.com. The "NIV" and "New International Version" are trademarks registered in the United States Patent and Trademark Office by Biblica, Inc.·

ISBN: 9780718096465 (HC)
ISBN: 9780718096489 (eBook)

Library of Congress Control Number: 2017930581

Printed in the United States of America

17 18 19 20 21 LSC 6 5 4 3 2 1

ABOUT Leadership⚹Network

Leadership Network fosters innovation movements that activate the church to greater impact. We help shape the conversations and practices of pacesetter churches in North America and around the world. The Leadership Network mindset identifies church leaders with forward-thinking ideas—and helps them to catalyze those ideas, resulting in movements that shape the church.

Together with HarperCollins Christian Publishing, the biggest name in Christian books, the NEXT imprint of Leadership Network moves ideas to implementation for leaders to take their ideas to form, substance, and reality. Placed in the hands of other church leaders, that reality begins spreading from one leader to the next . . . and to the next . . . and to the next, where that idea begins to flourish into a full-grown movement that creates a real, tangible impact in the world around it.

NEXT: A LEADERSHIP NETWORK RESOURCE COMMITTED TO HELPING YOU GROW YOUR NEXT IDEA.

LEADNET.ORG/NEXT

CONTENTS

DEDICATION

I have the distinct privilege to travel the globe to consult with outstanding leaders in ministry and the marketplace, speak at conferences, teach at leadership roundtables, and influence organizations for a dramatically better future.

None of that would be possible without two of my team members who understand *Bigger, Faster Leadership*. In fact, they personify it. They are my two daughters. They continually assess opportunities and align our resources for greater impact. Every day and in every way, they live by the theme of this book: your size and speed are controlled by your systems and structures.

Rachel and Debbie are my dear daughters, brilliant business partners, and heartfelt encouragers.

Thanks, love, and more to come—bigger, faster.

INTRODUCTION

Bigger. Faster. Bigger and faster. Business executives, pastors, and leaders of nonprofits all want their organizations to have greater size and speed. They need to understand the fundamental principle that drives more rapid growth. It's a principle I discovered a few years ago on a surprising afternoon.

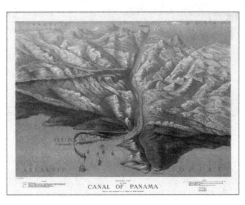

LIBRARY OF CONGRESS

I had never been to Panama City, but in January 2013 I was invited to speak at a conference there. With two friends, Maury Davis and J. Don George, I arrived on a flight that landed a day before the first session of the event, so we had plenty of time to see the sights. Maury and Don had been to Panama several times before, and they asked if I wanted them to take me on a personal tour of the Panama Canal. To be honest, I was very excited about seeing something I had heard about my whole life.

An hour or so later, we stood in the pleasant midday sun on an observation deck, watching some of the biggest ships on earth entering and leaving locks whose gates looked like skyscrapers. The hulls of the ships were only a few feet away from each side. I instantly realized this was an engineering marvel—a wonder of the world.

I could have stayed and stared at the ships for hours, but Don and Maury had more for me to see. They took me to the museum that told the amazing and complex history of the canal. As I absorbed the way the canal was built, it dawned on me that I was looking at one of the most important leadership principles I'd ever discovered: the size and speed of the ships are completely controlled by the systems and structures created by the engineers and the workmen.

I learned that the Panama Canal wasn't just a nice idea; it was an economic necessity. For centuries, explorers, kings, presidents, and business leaders tried to find a way to shorten the trip from the Atlantic to the Pacific. Crossing the narrow isthmus of Central America offered plenty of promises, but it proved to be a daunting challenge. Still, the hardships seemed worth the risks. By that day in January, the cost of taking a cargo ship through the canal was about $500,000 compared to the $3 million it cost to travel around the southern tip of South America and up the other side of the continent. For executives of shipping companies, success is defined clearly and simply: moving cargo economically and quickly from port to port—in this case, from a port on one ocean to a port on another.

> The size and speed of the ships are completely controlled by the systems and structures.

For more than a century in every step of the excavation, construction, and operation of the canal, politicians and engineers lived with the creative tension of vision, control, and submission. The leaders tapped into the talents of many different experts, and they used three different water features: the oceans, a lake, and a river. Diversity and creativity weren't obstacles; they were necessities.

Wherever I go, leaders in churches, nonprofit organizations, and businesses tell me privately, "Sam, something is missing, but I can't put my finger on it. There must be something more." They feel vaguely discouraged their organizations aren't growing bigger and moving faster, but they can't find an adequate solution to their dilemma. And that day with my two friends at the Panama Canal gave me a dozen fresh insights about leadership. I jotted down a lot of notes as I stood on the observation deck and walked through the museum that afternoon, and I realized more passion isn't the answer, and bigger dreams aren't always the solution. Every leader is asking two questions: How can we grow? and How can we grow faster? The only way organizations can grow bigger and move faster is by accelerating the excellence of their systems and structures.

As I've shared what I learned at the canal, some people may have wondered, "How did he get all these leadership principles from looking at water and concrete?" There's an easy answer. When a painter walks into a house, he notices the quality of the paint job in every room. When a mechanic rides in a friend's car, he hears minute sounds that tell him volumes about the car's condition. When a doctor talks to a stranger, she notices details of the person's appearance that may signal undetected health concerns. When a musician listens to a song, she hears vocal notes and tonal qualities of instruments few of us ever notice. And when Sam Chand walks through life, everything relates to leadership—even the latest movie, a casual conversation, or a visit to the Panama Canal.

> The only way organizations can grow bigger and move faster is by accelerating the excellence of their systems and structures.

Within ten minutes of standing on the observation deck and watching the slow and steady movement of ships and locks, the synapses in my brain started connecting what I was seeing with fresh principles of leadership. By the time I walked out of the museum, I had at least a rudimentary understanding of the amazing process required to engineer and build such a colossal structure. I was especially intrigued by the fact that though the first efforts to dig the canal were performed mostly by hand and steam power, technology has advanced so much over the years that the locks and ships now move seamlessly according to digital input.

The history of the canal, as we'll see, is a story of monumental challenges, crushing failure, enormous obstacles, and stunning success. There were periods when collaboration broke down completely, but also times when progress rode a wave of outstanding cooperation. During the work, some partnerships that had originally begun with great promise ended in bitterness and blame. Other partnerships proved to work incredibly well under severe conditions because leaders weren't primarily invested in their own egos.

The effectiveness of the Panama Canal affects ports around the world. When ships got larger and some were too big for the canal, it caused major problems for shippers. We might say, "When the Panama Canal sneezes, the ports of the world catch a cold." But the other side of the equation is also true: when the canal was widened in 2016 so it could accommodate the largest ships and tankers in the world, commerce accelerated around the globe. The American Association of Port Authorities has learned that US ports and their partners will invest nearly $155 billion on port-related freight and passenger infrastructure by 2020.[1] Savannah and Charleston—two ports near my home in Atlanta—need to dredge their channels and build new docks so they can welcome the biggest cargo ships afloat.

> The history of the canal, as we'll see, is a story of monumental challenges, crushing failure, enormous obstacles, and stunning success.

The principles I observed when I visited the Panama Canal help leaders at all levels of organizations. I consult with leaders around the world, and they all want their companies, churches, schools, and agencies to grow larger and more quickly. When I visit with these leaders, I act like a doctor reading a patient's vital signs. The patient may come in with a broken arm, but the doctor still takes the temperature, feels the pulse, and checks the blood pressure. In the same way, a leader may have called me with a nagging problem or a crisis, but I check the vital signs: I ask plenty of questions to discover the organization's health.

I begin by asking about the compelling need that the organization is designed to meet, and then I explore the operational systems: when, where, and how these needs are being met. I don't start with the structure, the organizational chart of people's roles. I can't accurately evaluate the people and their roles until I've thoroughly analyzed the systems. A leader may have a gifted, competent, and dedicated person who is failing because the system doesn't draw out her best.

The history and effectiveness of the Panama Canal is a metaphor that gives us a fresh way to think about leading our organizations. The canal's systems include the massive construction project that required feats of engineering never attempted before. The construction systems were followed by operational systems—the locks and gates, of course, but also the "mules" attached to the enormous ships that mechanically and precisely guide them along the narrow passages inside the locks—and increasingly, implementing the latest technology in all facets of the operation. The organizational structure in all phases of construction, operation, and expansion of the canal involved top leaders, but they have been effective only when these leaders have selected, trained, and supervised outstanding managers and tens of thousands of workers. It was—and still is—a massive enterprise.

> A leader may have a gifted, competent, and dedicated person who is failing because the system doesn't draw out her best.

The story of the canal provides insights that lead to fresh ideas and exciting options some of us may have not considered before. Many, if not most, leaders reading this book have created the systems and structures they use each day, so they may be resistant to changing them. I'm not going to force anyone to change. Instead, I'll try to present a compelling motivation for all of us to look more closely at *what is* and be more courageous to step toward *what might be*. Perhaps the most important feature of this study will be the questions I'll ask you to consider. Great questions are worth their weight in gold because they invite us to think, dream, and dare to accomplish great things.

Too often, leaders become focused on the wrong questions, which inevitably lead to misguided solutions. When we concentrate on systems and structures, we're "majoring on the majors." Will there be questions about money, facilities, programs, and schedules? Of course, but those are secondary concerns. The most important issues—the ones that determine real success—are always about systems (including the processes of the budget, building, programs, manufacturing, marketing) and structures (the people in the organizational chart who implement the processes). When Jim Collins wrote in *Good to Great* that leaders need to get the right people on the bus, he was right. But first, you must have the bus! That's the system. The "right people on the bus, the wrong people off the bus" is the organizational structure.[2]

The principles I learned from the Panama Canal apply to every kind of organization. After I told a friend, whom I'll call Rick, what I'd learned, he had dinner with Phil, a man who had recently retired from an executive position in a major manufacturing firm.

> Too often, leaders become focused on the wrong questions, which inevitably lead to misguided solutions.

As soon as my friend explained that the size and speed of an organization depend on the systems and structures, Phil immediately said, "That's the difference between our company and our top competitor. The leaders at our company never focused on creating outstanding systems and structures. The leaders at the other company created a strong culture with effective systems of operation, and they hired and trained people exceptionally well."

My friend was surprised by Phil's instant understanding of the principle and his analysis of the two companies. My friend asked, "How did the top managers at your company lead?"

Phil grimaced a bit and answered, "They always looked for heroes."

My friend asked, "How did that go?"

"They ran out of heroes," Phil said as he shook his head. "It wasn't an effective management philosophy or practice."

You're a leader because you want to make a difference, and you want to have a growing impact on others. You want more size and speed for your organization. In this book, I'll help you create better systems and structures that will help you get where you want to go and get there more quickly. You're already a gifted, dedicated leader. I want to make you a more effective one.

You'll see this statement often in the book: *The size and speed of an organization are controlled by its systems and structures.* Don't miss its importance.

At the end of each chapter, you'll find some questions to stimulate your thinking and provide opportunities for your team to discuss the content. Don't rush through these questions. Explore them, ponder the implications, and find solutions that work for you, your team, and your organization.

CHAPTER 1

HOW DO YOU DEFINE THE NEED?

I n any business, church, or nonprofit organization, a clear definition of the need is essential to produce a compelling motivation to succeed. Entrepreneurs notice a gap in the market they can fill by creating a new company or a new product. Pastors are gripped by the reality that a segment of their community hasn't been reached with the gospel of grace. Visionary leaders are moved with compassion to establish nonprofit

Vasco Núñez de Balboa
LIBRARY OF CONGRESS

organizations to meet the needs of distressed people. In each organization, success is defined simply and succinctly. If it's too complex, it can't capture the imaginations of staff teams, employees, and volunteers—and it won't touch the hearts of those they're trying to impact.

Throughout history, compelling needs have always inspired bold action. Christopher Columbus convinced King Ferdinand and Queen Isabella of Spain to fund his quest for a water route to the Spice Islands off the coast of Asia. For decades, Portuguese explorers had sailed south around the Cape of Good Hope at the tip of Africa and across the Indian

1

Ocean. Each time they returned, they brought troves of magnificent spices and they made millions for their sponsors. However, the voyage around Africa's Cape of Good Hope and into the Indian Ocean was long and dangerous. Portuguese explorer Vasco da Gama's round-trip to India lasted more than two years, from July 1497 to August 1499. Columbus believed the western ocean, the Atlantic, was small and he could reach Asia in only a few short weeks of sailing.

The rivalry between Spain and Portugal was fierce, so the Spanish crown was eager to find a shorter, quicker, more profitable route to Asia. Columbus set sail on August 3, 1492. A little more than two months later, as his men were giving up hope of finding land and surviving the trip, his lookout spotted an island. Columbus was sure they had arrived at the coast of Asia. He called the natives "Indians."

> Compelling needs have always inspired bold action.

For several months, his three small ships sailed the Caribbean, landing on Hispaniola and Cuba. He returned to Spain in March of the following year with spices, gold, and a few "Indians," leaving thirty-nine men to form a colony on Hispaniola. When Columbus arrived at court, he was hailed as a hero and named "Admiral of the Ocean Sea."

Columbus returned on his second voyage later that year, but he discovered all the men he had left behind had been slaughtered by the natives. Undeterred, he explored more islands in the Caribbean. He was still convinced he was just off the coast of China, Japan, or India. Subsequent voyages failed to discover the riches of Asia, but the greed of the monarchs inspired them to finance more explorations. Columbus assured them vast stores of gold were waiting to be discovered, but little gold was found. Instead, shipwrecks, disease, and death surrounded his efforts to explore and colonize the lands he discovered. In 1504, when Columbus returned to Spain after his fourth voyage, the king and queen grew suspicious that he hadn't reached Asia at all, and they refused to fund any more of Columbus's expeditions. It became apparent that Columbus had succeeded in discovering lands no one in Europe knew existed. He hadn't found Asia; he'd found the Americas.

During these years, Columbus wasn't the only captain on the seas. Other explorers sailed to America under different flags, and gradually two American continents began to take shape on maps of the New World. In 1511, Spanish conquistador Vasco Núñez de Balboa played an important role in establishing the first lasting settlement on the continent of South America at Darién on the Isthmus of Panama. As it was for many other Spanish leaders, gold was more important than friendships to Balboa, so he treated natives harshly in his quest for riches. In September, two years after the settlement was established, he led a force of 190 soldiers and hundreds of natives into the jungle to find more gold. When he climbed a mountain, he looked south and saw a vast, calm ocean. He called it Mar del Sur, the South Sea. Others called it the Pacific Ocean.

The business of exploring, it seems, was hazardous. Like Columbus's, Balboa's ambition stirred up trouble for him and for those who followed him. King Ferdinand appointed a nobleman named Pedrarias as governor of Darién. The two men didn't trust each other, but they negotiated a tentative peace that lasted for several years. In 1517, Balboa began an incredible adventure. He built and then disassembled a fleet of ships so his men could carry the parts across the mountains, put them together again, and conquer all the lands bordering the South Sea.

By this time, however, Pedrarias had lost favor in the Spanish court, so King Ferdinand sent a new governor with powers to arrest and try Pedrarias in court. Pedrarias was afraid Balboa would testify against him, so he had him arrested and tried for treason. The trial was a kangaroo court. Balboa and four of his lieutenants were found guilty and summarily beheaded. False accusation and quick execution ended Balboa's drive to reach and explore the vast new ocean.

During this time of upheaval in Darién, another explorer was searching the South Atlantic for a route to the Pacific. Ferdinand Magellan was sure South America didn't extend very far south, so an easy route to the East could be found. However, his small fleet was disappointed in bay after bay along the eastern coastline. Only when they had reached farther south than anyone imagined they could go did they find a perilous route to the South Pacific. After months of sailing northwest without sighting land in the vast Pacific, Magellan and his men were reduced to eating rawhide straps. Many died of starvation before they reached the islands later known as the Philippines. Magellan made friends with a chief on one of the islands, but the intrepid explorer died in an ill-advised attack on a rival chieftain. Only one of his ships made it back to Spain—barely afloat and with a few ghostlike men on board. He had found a water route to Asia, but he also proved it was terribly long and dangerous to travel around Cape Horn. A path across the narrow isthmus of Central America was incredibly alluring, but it remained maddeningly elusive.

In 1850, more than three hundred years after Balboa and Magellan, Dr. Edward Cullen suddenly announced he had found an easy route from Darién to the Pacific. Several countries were very interested in following up on this discovery. They planned a joint effort, but US Navy Lieutenant Isaac Strain arrived with his ship before the others, and he refused to wait. He led twenty-seven men into the jungle. He was sure he would pick up Cullen's path very quickly, so he instructed his men to pack only a few days' rations. Forty-nine days later, Strain staggered out of the jungle on the Pacific side, starving and almost naked. He and his men had encountered thousand-foot mountains and suffered impenetrable jungles, drenching rains, oppressive heat, and the utter absence of resources. Seven of Strain's men died. Still, Dr. Cullen continued to insist his easy route existed, and many believed him.

In the next few decades, several countries sent teams of surveyors to find a workable route. The need to secure a shorter, inexpensive, workable shipping route between the Atlantic and the Pacific was still compelling. In fact, with far more ships on the seas, the need was greater than ever.

THE NEED CREATES THE VISION

Vision isn't born in a vacuum. A leader's vision is the result of being gripped by a palpable need. Who is being bypassed in our community? Who is in trouble and desperately needs help? What products do people want and need? What are the opportunities that aren't being realized, and what are the challenges holding people back? Ferdinand and Isabella desperately wanted a trade route that would enable them to compete with the Portuguese for the spices of Asia. Centuries later, the California gold rush caused tens of thousands to look for the quickest way to the west coast of America. Similarly, the imaginations of today's leaders are captured by a challenge or an opportunity.

The need propels the *what* and *why* questions, which shape the leader's vision. After the vision becomes clear, the next question I ask is always: "Who do I need to help me meet this need and make the vision a reality?" It's never *how, when, where,* or *how much.* I don't think about buildings, budgets, or schedules until I've found the indispensable human resources: a

> After the vision becomes clear, the next question I ask is always: "Who do I need to help me meet this need and make the vision a reality?"

mentor, a coach, or a model I can follow. I ask, "Who has experience I can draw from?" "Who is doing it well right now?" "Who has learned the most important principles I need to apply?" "Who can connect me with the best available resources?"

When I meet with leaders in business and the church who are starting new ventures, I encourage them to find the best human resource to help them early in the process. Only then is it time to ask how, when, where, and how much. In other words, who is an expert that can help them organize their systems and structures to meet the need and fulfill the vision for size and speed?

LOOK AT SYSTEMS AND STRUCTURES

When I talk to people who have been leading for a long time, I notice many of them are frustrated. Business leaders may tell me, "We have good products and a good sales team. Our manufacturing is doing well, and our warehouse gets products out on time. I can't understand why our company isn't growing faster." Similarly, pastors confide, "We have a talented worship team, people say they like my messages, and we have plenty of good programs. So why are we still stuck at three hundred people?"—or two thousand or wherever their growth has been arrested.

They're telling me they're not happy with their size and speed, but they keep doing the same things repeatedly, hoping the results will magically change the next time. But it's not the same things—in their frustration, they try to work harder, they ask more from their people, they're a little more intense, and they desperately search for the "missing ingredient" of success. None of these solutions provides more than a fleeting promise of change. In most cases, they're not asking the right questions.

Instead, they need to step back to analyze their systems and structures. If they improve these, size and speed almost inevitably follow. Systems aren't just buildings, programs, products, and budgets. They are *processes* that create and use buildings, programs, products, and budgets to facilitate growth and change. The systems include the organization's platforms, communication tools, and training devices to impart vision, inspire hope to meet the need, and enlist passionate involvement. When the commitment for systems to excel takes root in an organization, every planning meeting, every leadership event, every building, every dollar, and every communication becomes saturated with meaning. The organization's systems become well-oiled, powerful machines to accomplish great things.

> Systems aren't just buildings, programs, products, and budgets. They are *processes* that create and use buildings, programs, products, and budgets to facilitate growth and change.

The structure is the organizational chart of people who work together. We don't just fill in boxes on a chart. We find passionate, skilled people who see the system as an essential tool to meet the compelling need and make the vision a reality.

Systems and structures are inextricably related, and they enable the organization to reach out to touch their community. The beating heart of an organization's systems is the set of connections leaders have with their audience. Do the customers, the people in the congregation, or the needy people in the community believe the organization cares about them? How do we connect with people in the community or our customers? How do we recruit employees and volunteers? How do we develop leaders? Has the senior leader created a culture where employees, staff teams, administrators, and volunteers are enamored with the vision? The real issue isn't, "Can our people repeat the vision statement?"—though that's a major hurdle for many organizations. It is, "Do they *own* it? Does the need captivate their hearts and motivate them to move heaven and earth to make a difference?" If people are genuinely gripped by the vision, they'll use the systems to effect change.

Ultimately, all questions are people questions. How do we touch them? How do we draw them in? How do we empower them? How do we make decisions so everyone feels heard and understood? How do we celebrate their accomplishments?

"NOTHING'S HAPPENING"

I've talked to many leaders who have put in plenty of time and sweat, but they haven't seen the progress they envisioned. They've invested years in pumping up their troops and trying to find the next best thing to propel growth, but they've experienced frustration after frustration. Oh, they've seen a blip of progress here and there, but they want so much more. They've told themselves, "We're building quality, and quantity will eventually come." But now they're starting to doubt their own cheerleading. Yes, they've improved in a lot of ways, but the needle of progress hasn't moved perceptibly.

These leaders might complain, "Nothing is happening," but that's seldom the case. Quite often, some very good things are happening: customers are buying products and people are finding forgiveness and purpose in Christ, but the sales chart isn't moving up and to the right, and the back door of the church is so big there are as many people leaving as are coming. These leaders are saying, "The size and speed of this organization aren't what I hoped they'd be!"

One of the ways to understand the life cycle of any organization is to identify the current position in the order of five distinct phases:

- The *entrepreneurial* (discovery) phase is the exciting beginning, when every dream seems possible.
- The *emerging* (growth) phase is when the vision begins to take definite shape, leaders are empowered, and the organization sees real progress.
- The *established* (maintenance) phase is a time when leaders take a deep breath, enjoy their success, and watch their systems function well. But this phase is also dangerous because it can easily lead to complacency.
- The *erosion* (survival) phase is evident when the organization shows signs of decline, and the earlier vision seems unreachable.
- The *enterprising* (reinvention) phase is the result of a deeper grasp of the need, a renewed vision, fresh enthusiasm, and new strategies to meet the need. Giving an existing organization a fresh charge of vision and energy is difficult, but it's essential for future flourishing.[1]

This life cycle of organizations is true in this exact order for businesses, churches, shopping malls, neighborhoods, marriages, and every other type of human enterprise.

The two points when it appears that "nothing's happening" are in the entrepreneurial and erosion phases, but the two are emotionally and psychologically opposites. In the beginning, nothing is happening, but the leader is filled with hope and energy. Conversely, when the life is sucked out of the leader and the organization in the erosion phase, hope is a distant memory, and it takes tremendous willpower to get up and go to work each day. Prolonged stagnation can be a slow-release poison for the soul.

During these long, dark days of erosion, it's difficult for a leader to keep casting a compelling vision. He may not believe his own promises anymore! For a long time, he keeps smiling and saying what he has said for so long. He keeps self-doubt to himself, and in fact, he may not even recognize the creep-

> The two points when it appears that "nothing's happening" are in the entrepreneurial and erosion phases, but the two are emotionally and psychologically opposites.

ing pessimism in his thoughts. Sooner or later he thinks, *Maybe I just don't have it anymore. Maybe I'm not the right person to lead this organization.* But he may try to escape these inner conflicts by wondering if other people are the problem: *If only our board did a better job. Why can't my executive staff do anything right? Do I even have the right people? No, I'm sure I don't!* The leader may shift responsibility to anyone and everyone but himself. Initial confusion (*I don't understand what's going on*) often leads to negative conclusions: self-doubt and blaming others.

At every point in the phases of an organization's existence, leaders need to step back and ask the bigger questions about systems and structures. The fulfillment of their initial hopes for size and speed depends on putting these elements in place, and the turnaround from erosion to enterprising depends on them taking a hard look at their existing systems and structures and making bold, new decisions. For example, instead of assuming you made a bad hire, it might be more productive to assess the process you used: how well you selected, trained, and empowered the individual to thrive in the system and structure of the organization. Did you hire to meet a need in the system, and did you communicate the specifics of how your new hire would contribute to meet the fundamental need and fulfill the vision? Did you make the "win" crystal clear to him or her?

If you hire an executive for a department of a manufacturing company, what production goals did you set for this person? If you hire a youth pastor, did you make it clear that you expect growth in multiple areas, such as a specific goal in overall attendance by a certain date, the number of volunteers, the level of parent involvement, communication to students and parents, and the number of students who go to summer camp? The goals of increased size and speed are the result of creating and expanding the system and structure in the business, the nonprofit, or the church—and the new hire needs to see the clear connection. Too often, people we hire don't understand how they fit in. We just hire them and hope for the best. This strategy may work for a few bright people who take a lot of initiative, but not for most.

The task of leadership, then, isn't just to give people goals, but to help them utilize effective systems and structures to reach those goals. When we give lofty goals without the underlying framework, we create confusion and pressure—and sometimes despair and panic.

The other side of the equation is that some leaders get so fixated on fine-tuning their existing systems and structures that they forget the need and the vision. For instance, the recent trend in education is long-distance learning, which means online classes. Some educators dug in their heels for years because they were wedded to people showing up in their classrooms several times a week. But the goal of providing quality education at a reasonable cost for busy people created a revolution in the delivery system. The need shaped a new, clear vision, which drove innovation in the systems and structures.

Many businesses and churches have fallen in love with "the way we do things around here," so they seldom if ever evaluate systems and structures according to the pressing need and the compelling vision. Culture changes, and delivery systems become antiquated in a hurry. We need to stay alert and nimble, always keeping the vision fresh and open to creative new ways of fulfilling it.

CLIMBING OUT OF STAGNATION

At two points in the history of the Panama Canal, officials of the Canal Authority realized they had entered a prolonged stagnant phase, and they needed to make dramatic changes. The first major reconstruction happened in the years before World War II when the new class of larger American battleships required bigger locks. This effort was stopped because officials realized it wouldn't be completed in time for the battleships to use it before the war ended. The second expansion was finished in the summer of 2016, a $5.25 billion effort to expand the canal, enabling ships more than two and a half times the size of the previous limit to pass through the waterway.

The expansion of the canal had ripple effects in the ports on both coasts of the United States and around the world. A bigger and better system at the canal created a bigger vision, more investment, a higher level of activity, and greater profits for the shipping industry across the globe. Before this expansion, the Panama Canal was losing relevance and traffic; today it has a greater impact than ever before. It had become stagnant, but it is stagnant no longer.

If you feel stuck and your solutions are only creating more tension and frustration, I want to offer some words of encouragement:

- *You aren't alone!* You're in good company! You aren't the first person to feel as though your organization is in a rut, and you won't be the last. Others have found a way out of the quagmire of stagnation, and you can too.
- *The solution isn't as difficult as you might think.* Sure, you've tried a dozen different "surefire" answers, and none of them brought lasting change. But this time I'm suggesting a different way of looking at your organization and your role as the leader.
- *Identify the need your organization is designed to meet, and clarify the vision to meet it.* Yes, you've probably said it a thousand times before, but is it fresh to you? Do you own it? Let it keep you awake at night again with stunning possibilities.
- *Next, conduct a thorough analysis of your systems and structures.* How are decisions made? How does communication happen? Who has authority and responsibility? Which programs are vital, and which are just nice things to do? Who is passionate about meeting

the need and fulfilling the vision? Who has lost zeal and energy? My guess is that you'll uncover the problem through this analysis. The systems that brought you to this point may not be the ones to take you to where you believe God wants you to go. Be ruthless with the analysis. It'll pay off soon.

- *Stop doubting yourself, and stop blaming your people.* An undercurrent of discontent always surfaces in one way or another, often in passive-aggressive behavior. We smile as we point out others' errors—not to help them, but to make sure others know *we* aren't the problem.

- *Don't assume you have a powerful and positive culture.* Work hard to create the kind of environment where people thrive. An organization's culture—ranging from inspiring to stagnant to toxic—is created moment by moment and conversation by conversation in messages that communicate meaning and value.[2] Every planning meeting, every board meeting, every performance review, and every interaction of any kind imparts a message about what and who we value. In communication, words carry far less impact than gestures and body language. In the same way, how leaders act communicates more loudly and clearly than the words they say. And the topic and frequency of our celebrations speak volumes about our goals, our hearts, and our willingness to share the spotlight with others.

- *Match your stated values with your allocation of time, money, and attention.* Our people are watching. If we say our people are our greatest asset, but those who work closely with us feel ignored or used, we've sent a loud message that we can't be trusted. But if our hearts genuinely break for people in need and we take time to show love to the men and women we see each day, the people around us will believe what we say about caring for others.

- *Look closely at the visible symbols of the organization's culture, such as titles, office allocation, and other perks.* Are leaders held aloof from the rest of the organization, and how approachable and vulnerable are they? These symbols are declarations of values, culture, integrity, and care.

When we understand that size and speed depend on our systems and structures, we'll pay closer attention to the way things operate and how people are empowered and valued. When we feel stuck, we won't just put our heads down and try harder, hoping for a different outcome. Of course, we'll need tenacity and grit, but we'll add wisdom, insight, and hope to our determination.

> The systems that brought you to this point may not be the ones to take you to where you believe God wants you to go.

The interplay of systems and structures creates and sustains the culture—for good or ill. If I walk into any organization, it only takes a few hours, or at most a couple of days, to discern how things really happen. Leaders may tell me how their systems and structures work, but I may notice that a person low on the organizational chart is a power broker. Who can people see without an appointment, and who has an assistant with a calendar barricading the door? Who has influence across departments? Who is creating silos that block communication and creativity? What's the difference between the stated goals of the organization and what's celebrated? What do the leaders consider the real wins? For instance, some leaders get more excited about programs staying under budget and being completed on time than they do the human impact of those programs. And some care more about minimizing conflict on their team than about the team's effectiveness.

No matter how clearly the leaders draw the lines of responsibility, authority, and decision-making, a shrewd observer may discover there are a few people who make the most important decisions. If employees don't recognize this fact, they can go up the chain of command but be confused when people in positions of authority don't—or can't—make decisions. But if they realize the boss relies heavily on Sarah, a middle manager, they are wise to first go to Sarah to get her input and support. Then they can go to the boss and say, "I've already gotten Sarah's feedback, and she thinks this is a good thing to do." The boss then gives approval more readily. It's all in knowing how the *real* system and structure work in the organization. You can't work the system if you don't understand how it operates.

I sometimes hear people say, "I don't want any politics in our office!" That's an impossible requirement. Politics is simply the expression of polity, the way people are organized to get things done. We often think of politics as part of our government, but every group of people—families, churches, clubs, and companies—has a way of making decisions and accomplishing tasks. It's naïve to think we can be free of politics, but it's wise to notice the subtleties of who makes decisions, how they are made, and how things are done.

Systems must continually adapt to the needs and opportunities of the moment. Static systems gradually lose relevance, but dynamic systems anticipate evolving needs. When I talk to leaders, some of them tell me, "This is how we do things," and I can imagine they've done things that way for a long time. But other leaders explain, "This is how we do things today, but we're always learning how to adapt so we can be more effective as we pursue our biggest goals."

Some leaders assume the procedures that worked in the past will continue to work in the future, and they become frustrated when they don't see growth. But other leaders know they need to periodically revisit each of the major systems in their organizations—sales, hiring, marketing, IT, leadership development, volunteer involvement, and so on—so they can stay sharp, relevant, and effective. Of course, some staff members or employees resist change, and they resist even the evaluation that may lead to change. Many others, however, catch the leader's optimistic, creative, visionary spirit and explore new ways to get things done.

STRATEGIC AND TACTICAL

Far too often, leaders and their teams move instantly from a concept to the tactical details, without giving thought to the strategic concerns of the need, systems, and structure. For instance, a pastor told his staff that he wanted to host a conference at the church. The next sentences were about when to set the date and who the speaker might be. No one bothered to ask, "What needs are we trying to meet? Who is our real audience? What is our definition of success?" No one painted a compelling picture of how a conference would change lives and propel growth. Casting vision is more than *what*; it must also include a clear and powerful *why* or the people involved will lack passion and the plans will be stiff and rote.

> Casting vision is more than *what*; it must also include a clear and powerful *why* or the people involved will lack passion and the plans will be stiff and rote.

I believe leaders need to ask and answer five key questions—in this order—when they start any venture, and they need to keep asking them if they expect their organizations to grow. Consider the need and the vision for the existence of your organization and ask the following:

1. *Is it sustainable?* Will it last? How long do I want it to last?
2. *Is it scalable?* Can it grow? How far?
3. *Can it be replicated?* How can it be reproduced? What parts must necessarily be replicated for growth to happen?
4. *Is it functional?* How will it be organized? How will we answer the questions of who, how, when, where, and how much? What will be the systems and structures?
5. *Is it compelling to others?* How will we communicate the vision and plan? How will we cascade the communication from the top leaders to each tier of influence and involvement?

The first three questions are big picture and strategic; the last two are specific and tactical. People who are starting businesses and planting churches need to begin with the strategic questions and work their way to the tactics. Most leaders of existing organizations spend virtually all their time on the tactical function and communication. They seldom step back to consider the bigger questions. That's perhaps the biggest reason their organizations stop growing—or grow more slowly than they'd like.

Let me summarize: Long seasons of stagnation can be mind-numbing. Instead of trying harder with the same systems and structures, I recommend conducting a thorough analysis: clarify the need and the vision so you're captured again by the what and the why, and then spend plenty of time figuring out how you can reconstruct your systems and structures so they can support more size and speed.

The explorers and traders of the world desperately wanted a route across the narrow Isthmus of Panama to cut almost eight thousand miles off the path from New York to San Francisco, but the need and the vision went stagnant for more than three hundred years. You and I don't have to wait that long to find a solution! Progress, however, is often messy and difficult. In the next chapter, we'll look at the first heroic but flawed attempt to connect the two oceans.

THINK ABOUT THIS

Reflect on these questions and discuss them with your team:

1. Why is it crucial to begin with a clearly defined, compelling need? What happens when an organization loses sight of the need that prompted its beginning?

2. How does it feel to be stuck in the stagnation phase of an organization? What mind games do people play there?

3. What are some reasons it's tempting to "do things the way we've always done them" without doing the hard work of regular analysis of systems and structures?

4. What are some of the unspoken but powerful parts of your system? How do these aspects of your system shape how things get done and the relationships on your team?

5. Take some time to consider the five strategic and tactical questions near the end of this chapter. What insights and new ideas came from this analysis? What needs to change?

Remember: The size and speed of an organization are controlled by its systems and structures.

CHAPTER 2

HOW DO YOU HANDLE COLOSSAL FAILURE?

O cean navigation had been crucial to the advancement of nations since the Middle Ages when Middle Eastern explorers opened trade routes to India, the Spice Islands, and Africa. Finding a safe and quick passage was the highest priority for maritime countries. Decades before Columbus, Balboa, and Magellan opened the gates to the East by traveling west, Portuguese explorers had painstakingly made progress down the western coast of Africa, around the Cape of Good Hope, and into the Indian Ocean. Portugal became fabulously wealthy because of the spice trade from India, the Moluccas, and Indonesia. Portugal's

Abandoned French Machinery
LIBRARY OF CONGRESS

successes had been the impetus that fueled the efforts of the Spanish royals, Ferdinand and Isabella, and Columbus, the ambitious Italian who sailed under their flag. Magellan had proven the globe could be circumnavigated, but his path to Asia was far too long and treacherous. For centuries, explorers dreamed of a different, easier route. The need to find a better way to the riches of Asia was still compelling.

The gold strike in California in 1848 reinvigorated interest in a quicker route from the crowded Northeast to the promise of California's riches. By the following year, a flood of forty-niners looked for a way west to the gold fields. Some traveled in wagon trains across the plains and mountains of the American West, but others took the long water route around South America. Speed was of the essence. The first ones to the gold fields had the best chance to become wealthy.

To cut weeks off the trip to California, in 1850 engineers began to build a small railroad along the Chagres River and over the mountains in Panama to reach from Panama City on the Pacific to Monkey Hill on the Atlantic. Construction was supposed to take two years, but it took almost five years and more than $6.5 million. The fare to cross the isthmus was twenty-five dollars for a first-class ticket. Investors had been worried their venture would fail because of the delays and extra costs, but it proved to be a profitable effort. Much of the gold taken from California streams, more than $700 million, was transported across the isthmus on the railroad and then by ship to the banking centers in the eastern United States. Still, the small cars on the railroad couldn't haul much freight. Something larger—much larger—was needed.

Almost on the other side of the world, sailors had long known a narrow strip of desert was all that separated the Mediterranean from the Indian Ocean. For centuries, traders had docked at the north end of the Red Sea, caravanned across the sands, and then loaded their goods on ships again to take them to ports around the Mediterranean. In the middle of the nineteenth century, Frenchman Ferdinand de Lesseps proposed a grand plan to dig a canal in the desert. After ten years of digging and dredging, the Suez Canal was opened on November 17, 1869. The water route from Europe to Asia had been reduced by months and thousands of miles. De Lesseps was a hero to his nation and to the thousands of French people who had invested in the venture and were enjoying fabulous returns.

Success in Suez renewed interest in a route in Central America. French and American survey parties carefully explored several possible routes across Panama and Nicaragua. President Ulysses S. Grant authorized seven expeditions between 1870 and 1875. Finally, in the year the Suez Canal was officially opened, the French trusted de Lesseps to perform another engineering marvel. He selected a route near Balboa's original trek across the isthmus, and thousands of satisfied French investors were again eager to risk their savings on a new venture.

De Lesseps proposed a sea-level canal like the one in Suez. The two geographies, however, are very different. Suez is flat and in a desert, with soil that was easy to remove. The continental divide in Panama is 361 feet above sea level, and the hills are steep with solid rock.

Construction began on January 1, 1881. De Lesseps's managers recruited and hired more than forty thousand laborers, most of them Afro-Caribbeans from the West Indies. Excellent and experienced French engineers were hired. The construction plan, however, was fatally flawed. The route would be crossed by the Chagres River fourteen times. De Lesseps planned to dam and divert the river, but he had only observed it during the dry season. In the rainy seasons, the tranquil river became a raging torrent, washing away anything in its path. Again and again dams burst, mudslides buried equipment and men, and then stagnant pools of water bred clouds of mosquitoes. In addition, the major excavation at the Culebra Cut was much more difficult due to landslides. Disease proved to be the scourge of the project. Within a few years, more than twenty-two thousand people had died of malaria and yellow fever, including five thousand Frenchmen.

In 1885, it was evident to the French engineers that the sea-level plan was doomed to failure. The construction of a series of locks on both sides of the project became the only option. Still, disease, flooding rains, landslides, and intense heat made progress very slow. After eight years, the funding was spent but the canal was only 40 percent complete. Thousands of French families—eight hundred thousand people—had invested their life savings in the project, expecting it to be as successful as Suez. When it went bankrupt, they lost everything. An inquiry revealed that 150 French deputies had been bribed to vote to fund the project. In 1893, de Lesseps and several others were tried and found guilty. His conviction was later overturned due to the statute of limitations—he was arrested more than three years after the crime had been committed.

In 1894, the French tried again to raise money and manpower to rescue their failed effort, but the public had soured on it by this time. The New Panama Canal Company tried to find a buyer for the equipment and the work that had already been completed. They asked for $109 million, but they found no takers.

By all accounts the cost of the French effort to dig and build the canal—in terms of human lives, the cost to investors, and the reputation of the engineers—proved catastrophic.

WRONG BENCHMARKS

In many ways and for many different reasons, leaders encounter deep disappointments. Failure always creates a crisis of confidence—of the leader in himself and of the people in the leader. The first task is to define failure in *your* context. Failure is missing the mark. In many cases, the mark—the goal, the vision, the expectation, or the timetable—was unrealistic. In the French attempt to build a canal across the Isthmus of Panama, the leader and the organization suffered a failure of foresight and preparation, not an organizational collapse. The authorities did, however, uncover a moral failure on the part of de Lesseps and his chief lieutenants. The engineering failure in Panama was coupled with personal and national disgrace.

Our conception of failure is often the result of comparison. All of us know, or at least know about, a pastor whose church has experienced phenomenal growth in a relatively short time, and we expect the same growth curve as we implement similar programs. Or a business leader adopts the methods of the most successful company in the field and is disappointed when the results aren't comparable. Comparison kills. At first it promises life and joy and success, but sooner or later it reaps discouragement and division as team members blame each other for falling short.

Comparison itself isn't always wrong, but we need to have the right benchmark of measurement. If I practice running sprints and get my time down to eighteen seconds over one hundred meters, I can be thrilled that I've accomplished my personal best. Wouldn't it be silly for me to be upset that I can't run that distance under ten seconds, like Usain Bolt?

> Our conception of failure is often the result of comparison. Comparison kills.

The ancient Corinthians were a jealous, selfish bunch—a lot like us. When Paul wrote his letters to them, he sternly corrected them for jockeying for position in the church. One of their biggest problems was comparison that led to unhealthy competition, divisions, and bitterness. Near the end of his second letter, Paul told them bluntly, "We do not dare to classify or compare ourselves with some who commend themselves. When they measure themselves by themselves and compare themselves with themselves, they are not wise" (2 Cor. 10:12).

I believe Paul and the Holy Spirit are saying the same thing to us today. At regional and global meetings, in magazine articles, and in newsletters and blogs, we learn about the leaders who are the very best at some aspect of ministry. The same high but narrow platform is given to leaders in business who excel in one area. We can celebrate their success and learn from them, but too often we internalize the conglomerate message that success in our world means being as good as *all* of them in *all* the areas they represent! Shouldering this inordinate pressure is, in Paul's understated language, "not wise" because it inevitably leads to either one of or both twin evils: pride or self-pity.

I've talked to many leaders who wistfully told me they believe their circumstances are all that's holding them back from monumental success. They often express their frustration in "if onlys." They say, "I know I could build a much bigger church [or company] if I could only move to Dallas [or some other major city]," or "I know my business would take off if only I could get a contract like the big dog in the industry has," or "If only we were in a warmer climate, I could get better staff." The solution may be different for these leaders, but the underlying assessment is the same: "I could be doing so much better if only this external circumstance would change."

Of course, this kind of discontent doesn't end with our private daydreams of better situations and staggering growth. We are like the Corinthians; comparison causes us to look around at the people who are more successful, and a root of resentment begins to take hold. We think, *Well, I'm a much better preacher than he is*, or *I know much more about streamlining manufacturing than she does*, or any of a hundred different permutations that we're getting a raw deal. These leaders often frame their desire for greener pastures as "God's calling."

We need to recognize the insidious nature of comparison that often lurks undetected in our minds and hearts, and we need to listen more carefully to the voice of God and enjoy the situation where he places us. I know pastors of churches of two hundred in small communities who are magnificently successful in their context. They are reaching people, involving them, retaining them, building godly character into them, and making an impact on the community. They are doing exactly what God has called them to do, and they are doing it with excellence. In the same way, I know business leaders who have small but outstanding companies. They provide excellent products and services, and they have created a thriving, supportive, creative culture in their offices. Success needs to be viewed in the context of our realities, not by comparing ourselves to the biggest and fastest-growing organizations in our fields.

As organizations mature, the original vision may be lost as leaders see success in many different areas. Gradually, the passion that gave them the impetus to begin their church or business is diluted and perhaps completely forgotten. It's wise for leaders to compare their current growth to their original vision, not the success of other leaders. The original, driving, God-given reason to start a church—or change the direction of an existing church—may have been to reach a certain segment of the community, to provide care for a particularly needy group of people, or to build multiplying disciples. A business

> We need to recognize the insidious nature of comparison that often lurks undetected in our minds and hearts.

may have begun with the idea of creating, producing, and selling the very best widgets on the planet.

The question is: What progress have you made in fulfilling *that* vision? If my original exercise goal was to run one hundred meters in eighteen seconds and I achieved it, I can be completely happy with my accomplishment, and I can be unthreatened by the fact that millions of people can run faster than me. I was running only against myself. I can marvel at Usain Bolt without a hint of envy or dissatisfaction. In the 2016 Summer Olympics, the sprinters who won silver or bronze were thrilled to receive their medals because they knew gold was out of reach with Bolt in the race. They, too, were running with lofty but realistic expectations.

If I were asked to select speakers for conferences, I'd choose the pastor who has a church of four hundred in a town of three thousand, and I'd invite a business leader whose company is known for excellence in two areas: its products or services and its corporate culture. These are the leaders who deserve a platform.

Disappointments can also occur from systemic failures. The pastor of a church of ten thousand lamented that though they had baptized more than eight hundred people last year, the church hadn't grown at all. He wondered, "What happened to those people? Why didn't they stay involved? We don't know where they went." After some honest discussions with his staff, they realized they needed to find a much better way to relate to people before, during, and after they choose to be baptized.

To use business terms, his church was very good at selling but not very good at providing attractive, personal services to retain customers. The church's systems and structures were built to attract people and invite them to make a decision, but they weren't effective in assimilation, discipleship, small groups, and involving them as volunteers. In other words, they need to rework their systems and structures to meet the deeper and long-lasting needs of people who express interest in Christ and the church.

Some failures, though, aren't problems with perception or systems. They're personal. De Lesseps failed in all three areas. His initial expectations of a sea-level canal proved to be unattainable, and he wasted enormous resources of people, time, money, and equipment on systems that couldn't do the job. The damage to his reputation, however, wasn't only that he failed in his efforts to build the Panama Canal. He was a marvelous success in Suez, but his moral failures—his involvement in corruption that eventually cost the life savings of hundreds of thousands of people in France—tarnished his name for all time.

The clear majority of the failures I see in my consulting role with pastors and business leaders are from misplaced expectations and faulty systems and structures. But some are much worse than these. Like de Lesseps, they are moral failures. I've known leaders who committed major indiscretions, embezzled funds, or became addicts. Because we believe in a God of grace, mercy, and power, we can say there are no "fatal failures"; but some of these flaws disqualify people from leadership positions, at least for a season, until they can prove they have been rehabilitated. Too little mercy is unlike our Lord, but too much mercy is blind, foolish, and fails to require true repentance.

> Some failures, though, aren't problems with perception or systems. They're personal.

The most important question about retaining or restoring a leader who has fallen in a significant way is this: Is there genuine sorrow, repentance, the desire for restitution, and a commitment to prove to be trustworthy over time? When there is humility, contrition, and patience to prove change is real, there is real hope for restoration to at least some role in the future. Where there is denial of responsibility, minimizing the damage, and impatience to resume a leadership role, we should be suspicious that change has even begun.

WHEN YOUR ORGANIZATION EXPERIENCES FAILURE

When the numbers turn down, unexpected setbacks happen, or conflict ravages an organization, some leaders immediately try to put the best face on it. They say, "Everything's fine," but plenty of people know it's not the truth, so the leader begins to lose an organization's most valuable commodity: the people's trust.

Whenever you experience organizational disappointments, speak the truth without any spin. Your people know when you're hedging the truth. They can sense it in your voice, and avoiding the painful truth for a day or a week does far more long-term harm than it does any short-term good. In the leadership meeting, share the sales figures, the budget numbers, the attendance, or whatever is the metric for your organization, and don't hedge an iota. Say, "Here's what's true," but also add, "And here's how we're doing compared to other organizations like ours." This comparison is helpful because it provides context. For instance, if you've seen a 10 percent decline and the average of other organizations is a 15 percent decline, you and your people can conclude you're doing something right. But if you've seen a 10 percent drop but others have enjoyed an increase, you should be honest about that truth.

Businessman Max De Pree famously noted, "The first responsibility of a leader is to define reality. The last is to say thank you. In between, the leader must become a servant and a debtor. That sums up the progress of an artful leader."[1]

Along with rigorous honesty about the present, the leader needs to be prepared to at least begin the conversation about a better future. He doesn't need all the answers, but he needs an idea or two to get the ball rolling. After presenting the cold assessment of reality, he can say, "I have a couple of ideas about what we can do, but first, I want your input." This conversation isn't an autopsy of the corpse of the grand vision that seems to lie dead on the office table. Instead, this is an invitation to participate in a resurrection. The question, then, isn't, "What went wrong?" but rather, "What can we do now to move forward?"

> Whenever you experience organizational disappointments, speak the truth without any spin.

When I've been in this situation, and I've been there more times than I can count, I've learned to say something like this: "The results are disappointing, but I believe we have what it takes to turn this around. Now, I'd like to hear your ideas before I share mine. We're all in this together, and we'll find a way through." One of the most important tasks for the leader in this conversation is to value and affirm the contribution of the team—not to blame them for the problem, but to include them in the solution, and include them in a way that honors and motivates them to give themselves heart and soul to the solution.

One of the things I often say after hearing my team's input is: "I'm so glad to hear your hearts and your creative ideas. In fact, I like your ideas better than mine. Now, let's talk about who needs to do what." The meeting may have started with a dose of painful reality, but I try to move them immediately to shared ideas and then to specific implementation so we'll see the desired impact.

In this conversation, and in dozens of others that happen individually and as a team in the coming days and weeks, leaders need to express again and again, "We can do better. We have what it takes. We have great ideas, and we have the right people to turn the corner and make progress. We can get where we need to go."

It's human nature to try to avoid any responsibility for failure by passing it to anyone and everyone. We throw blame against the wall of every person we know, and we hope it sticks somewhere. Good leaders assume more responsibility, not less. The disappointment may not be their fault, but it's their responsibility to help the team interpret the situation through the lens of hope and work together to make progress.

Wise leaders don't point fingers too eagerly at others. They may need to point out that a team member needs to perform better, but they don't communicate this message publicly or harshly. They are shepherds of people as well as leaders of organizations. Every disappointment, every setback, is an opportunity for people to grow, learn, change, and develop deeper wisdom and better skills. Failure is seldom a catastrophe unless we see it as a catastrophe.

OVERCOMING OBSTACLES

Ferdinand de Lesseps encountered obstacles on the Isthmus of Panama that were far more daunting than he expected. He had encountered intense heat in Suez, but not combined with drenching rains, swarms of mosquitoes, fatal diseases, and incessant mudslides. In the dry climate of the Egyptian desert, equipment suffered from overexposure to sand and dust, but in Panama, parts rusted within days. Gigantic earth-movers often sat as motionless hulks, stuck in the mud or incapacitated by rust—and they

> Failure is seldom a catastrophe unless we see it as a catastrophe.

couldn't run down to the store to get a new part. Repairing and replacing equipment proved to be an overwhelming, time-consuming burden.

From my experience, and from my discussions with thousands of leaders over the years, I've seen people face—and, with courage and skill, overcome—many different obstacles. Let me identify and illustrate the most common ones.

The Dangers of Momentum

De Lesseps and the myriad of people in France who saw such grand success in Suez were intoxicated by momentum. For many leaders, past success blinds them to potential future problems. Momentum exaggerates our intelligence and skill, and it hides our weaknesses. Internal fractures go unnoticed, and they can cause major damage before anyone addresses them. In modern parlance, successful leaders too often drink their own Kool-Aid of greatness. It tastes good at first, but it makes us sick.

Where do we find these fractures? In churches, we need to look at the enthusi-asm and number of volunteers. They are "the canary in the coal mine." Canaries are very sensitive to poisonous gases, so

> For many leaders, past success blinds them to potential future problems.

miners often took them into the mines as an early warning signal. If the bird sang, the miners knew they were safe, but if the canary died, poison gas was present. When volunteers lose their passion, we'll find noxious gas in the core of the organization. We see the same phenomenon in businesses, but in third-level employees instead of volunteers. They are "the boots on the ground" connecting with suppliers and customers. Their commitment to excellence, or the lack of it, tells the leader everything about the culture of the company.

Measuring the Wrong Things

In our society, virtually everything has a number: our weight, our height, our blood pressure, our bank accounts, our houses, and our passports. In our organizations, we assign numbers to everything we deem important. We often, however, spend too much time and attention measuring the wrong things.

Pastors, boards, and leadership teams in churches traditionally focus on the ABCs: attendance, buildings, and cash. These are certainly important, but we often fail to measure factors that reveal the heart and health of our churches, such as the number of first-time guests, the proportion of guests to regular attenders, the conversion rate of guests who become regular attenders, the conversion rate of attenders who join small groups, and most important, the number of volunteers actively engaged in ministry. These factors reveal the "stickiness" of the church. Too often pastors become frustrated because they don't see overall growth, but they don't peel back the layers to measure and evaluate the crucial connections people need to make.

Similarly, in business, executives often look at the bottom line, but they need to observe and measure the intangible elements that lead to excellence, productivity, and tangible results. Corporations, especially in manufacturing, may to a large extent depend on machines, but the culture always is a function of human relationships. Corporate culture may not be strictly measurable, but it's certainly noticeable. Executives can keep an eye open to notice the level of creativity, commitment, and care in their managers and all levels of employees.

Losing Passion for the Vision

When I consult, I talk with people at all levels to feel the pulse of life. Quite often the top leaders are full of vision and passion, but those who are down the organizational chart often don't get up in the morning dreaming about how their role can change the world that day. They have tunnel vision, focused on their narrow role and their stated responsibilities. Maybe they didn't listen when the leader explained how their role is essential, or maybe the leader didn't make the point at all. When people can't connect the dots between their role and the grand vision, they spend time protecting their turf, daydreaming about other things, and just putting in their time. They aren't excited, creative, connected, desperate in prayer, or tenacious about making their lives count.

Unresolved Conflict

Disagreements are inevitable. When a couple says they've never argued, I wonder if they live in different states. In churches and in companies, the ability to argue agreeably is a sure sign of emotional health and organizational strength. The problem occurs in two ways: when disagreements are interpreted—or meant—as personal attacks, and when disagreements are allowed to fester into resentment. Most of us want to be known as nice Christians, so we don't usually come out with guns blazing when we're hurt and upset. Instead, we smile as we stab people in the back with gossip, and we build secret—or not-so-secret—alliances against the offender.

One of the most important tasks of a leader is to notice long-simmering conflict between team members and wade in to resolve it. Sadly, some leaders don't have the courage to make this move. They spiritualize and tell themselves they'll "trust God to give them love for one another." They forget that they are God's instruments to offer truth, correction, repentance, and reconciliation. When resentment is finally addressed, tensions initially rise, but there's hope for understanding, forgiveness, and true peace. Left alone, resentment becomes a cancer in the life of the team, and it metastasizes throughout the organization. At that point, the leader will wish he had done something a lot sooner!

Too Much Mercy

As people who have experienced the grace and mercy poured out on us in Jesus Christ, we're glad to express grace and mercy to others. It's irresponsible of us as believers, and especially as leaders, however, to ignore perpetual troublemaking and assume "it'll work out somehow." We have a responsibility to the team and the organization to take more decisive action.

All leaders wear two hats. Pastors wear the hats of a shepherd and a CEO; business leaders wear the hats of a coach and a boss. In both arenas, I've seen countless leaders who found excuses to wear only one hat. They may have avoided wading into the other person's life because they don't like conflict, or a past conversation blew up and ended badly. Whatever the cause, avoiding reality always creates much bigger problems—for the leader, for the team, and for the person who is incompetent or divisive.

Everyone occasionally has a bad day. That's not the problem. But when people habitually fail in their responsibilities or cause tension, we need to express "tough love" by stepping in to speak the truth and offer a path of growth and change. If a team member humbly receives our instruction, everybody wins. Real change always takes time, but we can be far more patient if someone has a positive attitude. If, however, the person rejects our message, blames others, makes excuses, or minimizes the severity, we need to acknowledge his or her unacceptable choice and begin the process of releasing that individual.

Failure to Leverage Peer Pressure

Americans have been amazed at the incredible skill, courage, dedication, and teamwork of SEAL teams. In conflicts in the Middle East, and perhaps in many other places we don't hear about, these intrepid warriors bring out the very best in each other as they accomplish the seemingly impossible. For years parents have warned their teenagers about the dangers of peer pressure, but SEAL teams show it can be a powerful and productive force that raises the level of productivity on the team and throughout the organization.

When teams in churches, nonprofits, and businesses have esprit de corps, everyone is creative and dedicated to accomplish the mission, everyone has each other's back instead of stabbing each other in the back, and everyone pushes each other to do their very best. In this environment, slackers have nowhere to hide. Team members don't wait for the leader to address the problem. They notice it quickly and speak to the one who's not pulling his or her weight. Handled in this way, small issues seldom escalate into major problems.

Great teams have systems and structures to create and intensify positive peer pressure. Regular reports in front of everyone encourage transparency, honesty, feedback, and better ideas. The systems continually clarify the team's mission and each person's expectations so they have no question about the vision or their individual roles in achieving it. This brings out exceptional performance in every member of the team.

Lack of Personal Improvement Plans

Corporate goals and targeted benchmarks of progress are essential for success, but leaders also need to implement personal improvement plans for each team member. Without them, staff members may wonder if they're doing a good job. In fact, they might even worry about their future in the organization. The personal investment of leaders in the lives of their team members shows acceptance, provides affirmation for a job well done, and allows the leader to give direct feedback on goals set in the last regular assessment. This connection encourages the team member's enthusiastic "buy in" to the leader's vision and the organization's goals.

Veteran employees need at least an annual review of corporate and personal goals, and new employees probably need quarterly reviews for the first year. In these meetings, both the staff member and the leader can give an analysis of progress and point out areas where improvement is needed. I always advise leaders to let the staff member set his or her goals for the coming year. Goals need to be specific and measurable. For example, an item on an administrative assistant's list of goals might include sending an agenda for the staff meeting, with assignments, to each person on the team by noon on the day before the meeting each week. (Yes, that specific!)

Self-assigned goals require a bit more time for the person and the leader to talk them through and clarify them, but they are more specific and more motivating than traditional, top-down reviews. Research has shown that self-management has higher returns than top-down assignments.

Responsibility Without Resources

When I talk to team members in churches, nonprofits, and businesses, I often uncover their frustration at being assigned a responsibility but lacking the resources to fulfill it. The resource they need may be tangible, such as money, staff, space, materials, or time; or it may be intangible, such as information, training, or connections to people they need to help them plan and execute the task.

Quite often communication has broken down somewhere. The team member may not have voiced the need very clearly, or the need was spoken but the leader became distracted by other priorities. Sometimes leaders have difficulty delegating to others, so they keep the responsibility and resources for themselves. This drives competent, gifted, and dedicated staff members crazy, and it erodes their confidence and competence.

Good leaders need to delegate clearly and efficiently. This means they clearly define the team member's responsibility and make sure all the resources are available to get the job done. This step is crucial. Excellence, trust, and productivity simply won't occur unless the leader takes time to ensure team members have adequate resources to fulfill their responsibilities and contribute to the organization's vision.

Deadlines Are Too Flexible

A vision without a plan is just a hope, and a plan without a deadline is only a wish. Deadlines are the specific markers of progress. I've watched as team members pushed back on a leader's stated deadline. Sometimes the interaction was good and necessary because an unforeseen obstacle forced a delay. But I've seen some leaders accept delays for no better reason than a staff member's poor planning and irresponsible behavior—and quite often poor planning and irresponsible behavior that had happened many times before but was never addressed.

> A vision without a plan is just a hope, and a plan without a deadline is only a wish.

When leaders allow this kind of behavior to dictate delays, they send a loud and clear message to that person and the rest of the team: "What I say doesn't matter!" When team members experience this one too many times, they realize the irresponsible person is running the team. They lose respect for the leader, and productivity plummets.

In every meeting and for every assignment, make sure you don't leave an item before you've clearly communicated *who does what by when*. This requirement isn't too rigid or demanding. It's necessary for people to work together effectively.

Lack of Support from Leaders

As I travel and meet with team members, many of them tell me, "I love my job, and I'm very committed to the work we're doing, but to tell you the truth, I feel invisible. I don't feel appreciated." They often quickly add, "I know that shouldn't be important, but I would be a lot more motivated if I felt valued."

We need to be our team's biggest cheerleaders—not faking it, but genuinely appreciating them and their contribution to the cause. We have big dreams and goals, but God has entrusted people to us, and these people need us to shepherd and coach them by celebrating them in countless ways. We thank them for their good work and their positive attitude, we notice an especially good job someone has done, we tell others about their contribution, and we stop to listen when they want to share an idea or concern. When things don't go well, we provide clarity with patience, we exhibit extraordinary optimism in the face of setbacks, and we help people get up when they fall. In all of this, we create an inspiring culture for the people God has given us to lead.

They Hate to Wait

Most leaders are consummate doers. They can't stand to wait—at stoplights, for reports, for phone calls, or for progress toward their goals. Much of life, however, happens "in the meantime." Something important—and probably unseen—is happening in you and your organization as you wait. The Bible uses the metaphor of sowing and reaping (James 5:7). Have you thought about the time between those events? It's a long time. The farmer may do some weeding and he may pray for rain, but he can't make the grain ripen any faster. If he tries to rush things, he may ruin the whole crop.

I believe God wants to teach us some of the most important lessons in the meantime, as we wait. We want certainty, but God wants us to trust him during the long seasons of ambiguity. If we are too anxious and impatient, we run the risk of resentment ("God, what's wrong with you?"), losing focus ("I wonder what I need to do now"), self-doubt ("What did I do wrong?"), or complacency ("What's the use?").

Throughout the Bible, God took his chosen leaders through prolonged times of silence and waiting. Noah, Abraham, Joseph, Moses, and the prophets often waited for decades for God to show them the next step in their journey. Is God's path for us any different? No, God uses times of waiting to prepare us just as he used those times in our forebears' lives.

When waiting feels like death, realize you're exactly where God wants you to be. Declare that his goodness, his wisdom, and his timing are right. Admit your distress; be honest with him about your frustrations. Develop a heart of waiting on the Lord, expecting him to open doors when the time is right. And demonstrate a heart of faith as you wade through your time of ambiguity.

Until we see Jesus face-to-face, disappointments will be part of life. We are wise to learn from others' mistakes so we avoid them, but alas, most of us aren't that smart. We only learn the hard way—by making mistakes and learning the lessons firsthand. No matter how we learn them, they are incredibly valuable. The rest of your life and your effectiveness as a leader depend on the lessons you learn from disappointments. A wise pastor told his leadership team, "The lessons you learn from your disappointments and failures before you're

> We are wise to learn from others' mistakes so we avoid them, but alas, most of us aren't that smart.

forty determine how God will use you for the rest of your life." That's a sobering and hopeful insight about the path and the purposes of God.

The French effort to dig and build a canal across Panama proved to be a colossal failure. For years, the scarred landscape lay silent, with only an aborted attempt by the French to renew the work. Finally, they admitted they couldn't do it. A new vision was needed, with a new source of energy and enthusiasm.

In the next chapter, we'll see that it took an extraordinary leader, one who was willing to push the limits of possibilities, to make it happen.

THINK ABOUT THIS

Reflect on these questions and discuss them with your team:

1. What are some ways comparison creates the wrong benchmarks for us? What are some good, right, and healthy benchmarks of progress for you and your organization?
2. What are some ways you can tell if your systems and structures have failed?
3. In times of disappointment, why is it important to communicate the hard truth but with optimism? What happens when leaders shade the truth so they'll look better? What happens when they communicate gloom and despair?

4. Pick two of the obstacles in the last section in the chapter. How has each been a hindrance to you? What are you going to do about them?

Remember: The size and speed of an organization are controlled by its systems and structures.

CHAPTER 3

WHERE DO YOU FIND FRESH PASSION AND PURPOSE?

Theodore Roosevelt didn't follow the standard script for people with his background. His father was one of the wealthiest and most respected men in New York. The family was in the top echelon of patricians. Like other young men of his class, Theodore attended an Ivy League school. When he graduated from Harvard, he was expected to live a life of leisure— reserved, distant, and protected from "those people" in the rest of society.

Roosevelt Sitting at the Controls of a Steam Shovel

LIBRARY OF CONGRESS

But Theodore Roosevelt was unlike anyone else. As a boy, he suffered terribly from asthma. He often had such trouble breathing that his father drove him around New York in a carriage in the middle of the night to get fresh air. But the boy was an avid naturalist. In college, he was a boxer. As a young man, he went out west, bought a ranch, and became a cowboy. He became an expert hunter and tracked trophy game for days so he could get a shot. But nothing prepared his family and friends for his most stunning decision: to enter politics. The fray of state and national government was considered beneath people of his breeding. He dropped out of Columbia Law School to run for office.

Roosevelt first ran unsuccessfully for mayor of New York, but this defeat didn't stop him. He was elected to the New York State Assembly from Manhattan, and he served two years, from 1882 to 1884. He then became police commissioner for New York, and he reformed the corrupt force. He was known for "unimpeachable honesty."[1] During this time, a journalist reported on the tragic plight of immigrants in the slums of the city. Roosevelt asked the journalist to take him for a firsthand look. He observed living conditions he had never imagined before. The experience turned Roosevelt into a compassionate and tenacious champion of the downtrodden.

Roosevelt was appointed assistant secretary of the navy in 1897, and he became dedicated to the effort to force Spain out of Cuba. When the US battleship *Maine* exploded in Havana harbor, Roosevelt readied the navy for war. He was never satisfied to sit on the sidelines, so he resigned from his role with the navy. He joined the army as the colonel of the "Rough Riders," who became famous for their charge up San Juan Hill, which was actually Kettle Hill. Like a few intrepid men, Roosevelt felt more alive with bullets passing close to him. Later he called that success "the crowded and glorious hour of my life."[2]

After the brief and successful war in Cuba, Roosevelt returned to the States and ran successfully to become governor of New York. His energy and skill in leadership captured the national attention of the Republican Party, and he was asked to become President William McKinley's vice presidential nominee for his second term. The pair won the election, but only months after the inauguration, an anarchist assassinated McKinley. The youthful Roosevelt suddenly became president of the United States.

Many seasoned political observers believed the inexperienced Roosevelt would be no more than a caretaker president. They were badly mistaken. He became an activist, busting the trusts that dominated business and strangled competition, resolving a crippling coal strike, regulating the railroads, and creating the Meat Inspection Act and the Pure Food and

Drug Act to stop the sale of rancid meat and tainted drugs. In addition, he created the United States Forest Service and established scores of national monuments, national forests, national parks, and game preserves. He gave powerful and popular speeches that captured the imaginations of the public, though his brilliant oratorical skills infuriated his opponents. He is often called "the first modern President,"[3] but he was unlike any other national leader before or since.

Not long after he became president, Roosevelt realized American military and industrial strength would be greatly enhanced by completing a canal across Panama. In a speech to Congress in December 1901, he announced his plans to finish the canal. He asserted, "No single great material work which remains to be undertaken on this continent is as of such consequence to the American people."[4]

Within months Roosevelt took action. He sent an emissary to begin negotiations with Colombia, since at the time Panama was a province of that country. When negotiations stalled, Roosevelt again took the initiative. He instigated a revolution in Panama and ordered his soldiers to bribe the Colombian soldiers to put down their rifles. Within hours the "battle" for Panama was over, and on November 3, 1903, Panama became a nation, with a constitution that had already been written by Americans who had anticipated the success of the revolution.

The new Panamanian government signed a treaty with the United States, and the Canal Zone was created. A few months later, Roosevelt authorized the purchase of the buildings and equipment from the remnants of the French company for $40 million. The grand project was on again!

TWO CRUCIAL QUESTIONS

When disappointment stalls a leader's plans, he or she often should craft a new vision and take bold action to move the organization forward. The courage to take an honest look at setbacks is essential. Leaders may be tempted to engage in gloom and despair, but they must find a way to see disappointments as turning points, not dead ends.

The French canal project was a disaster in every possible way. By the late 1800s, the dream of engineering a path across Central America seemed hopeless, but Theodore Roosevelt still believed. The need was as great as ever—even greater because trade had increased exponentially in the previous decades. When he became president, Roosevelt essentially asked two questions about the canal: Can we do this? And do we have the right people to accomplish it?

> Leaders find a way to see disappointments as turning points, not dead ends.

Perhaps no other leader in American history had as much self-confidence as Theodore Roosevelt. He had an indomitable, can-do spirit—even genuine joy in facing the biggest problems of his day. He had a powerful blend of optimism and tenacity. What was the source of these traits? He had overcome severe asthma as a child and a frail body as a young man. He had endured the death of his mother and his wife on the same day, just after the birth of his first child. These heartaches threatened to destroy him, but eventually they made him more resilient.

Where others saw defeat and doubt, Roosevelt saw opportunity. The French failure in Panama didn't scare him. He had complete confidence in American capabilities to go anywhere, face any challenge, and overcome every obstacle. His answer to the first question was undoubtedly, "Of course we can!" Like every great leader, Roosevelt never employed the word *enough*; for him, there was always "more."

When we experience significant setbacks, we may wonder if the dream is dead. We need to dig deep to find that blend of optimism and tenacity. We ask ourselves, "Is the need still there? Is the vision still alive? Can we find a way to fulfill it?" Halfhearted statements won't do. The people around us need to see in our eyes and hear in our voices affirmation that we still believe—we believe the need must be met, we believe we are the people who can lead the effort, and we believe in the people around us.

The second question is often much harder to answer. When leaders look at the people around them, they need to decide who to *retain*, who to *reassign*, and who to *release*. They consider each person's attitude and capacity—not how well a person fits in the current situation, but how well he or she fits in a specific role in the new, expanded vision.

I often use the metaphor of a ladder to illustrate the leader and a team. A person can climb only a few feet up a ladder with no one holding the ladder. He can climb higher if he has someone steadying it, but he can climb much higher if he has enough strong, attentive, skilled people holding the ladder. In fact, if he has the right people, he can get a much taller ladder. The question for every leader is, who is holding your ladder?

> Dig deep to find that blend of optimism and tenacity.

In my consultations with leaders around the world, I've noticed four kinds of people in their organizations: *wanderers* never see the vision, but they don't care; *followers* see the vision, but they don't pursue it on their own; *achievers* are gripped by the vision and are intrinsically motivated to take action; and *leaders* are compelled by the vision to gather others to pursue it with them. Leaders gather ladder holders. They can only climb as high as the number, dedication, and capacity of those who are holding their ladder.

- Wanderers
- Followers
- Achievers
- Leaders

No organization can grow if there are too many wanderers, but every organization has a fair share of followers. Most top leaders are thrilled to have plenty of achievers, but the best leaders know they can't reach their highest goals unless they find and cultivate other passionate, competent leaders to work alongside them.

THE HARDEST DECISIONS

Once a leader has a refreshed vision, he faces the toughest decisions: the ones about people. Decisions about projects, programs, schedules, and funding may seem difficult, but they're relatively simple compared to hard choices to retain most, reassign some, and release a few. We might assume the setback we've experienced caused the greatest dissonance in us and in our organizations, but we often face far greater chaos when we take steps to restructure our leadership teams.

Changing directions is relatively easy; changing people is excruciating. Some are eager to pour themselves into the renewed vision and the updated strategy, but others are wedded to yesterday's solutions, and they're more interested in protecting their own turf than in expanding their horizons. Some are confused and just need some time and attention to get on board, but others continue to resist long after we've given them adequate information and time. Give everyone a chance to buy into the vision, but watch for people who are chronically resistant, negative, and divisive.

> Changing directions is relatively easy; changing people is excruciating.

The drama of pursuing a new vision not only makes people in our organizations feel insecure; it makes us feel insecure too. We may want affirmation from the people who have questions about the new direction we're charting. When they aren't quick to dive in with all their hearts, we may wonder if they're with us—and we may wonder if we're even worth following. When they ask hard questions, we wonder if they're loyal. At a time when we're trying to build a stronger team, the new direction often creates hesitation, suspicion, and conflict.

We need to learn that agreement doesn't necessarily equate to loyalty, and disagreement doesn't necessarily mean the person is disloyal. In an atmosphere of trust, disagreements aren't interpreted negatively; they're just part of the process of fine-tuning the direction of the organization.

When a new vision is being presented over the course of days, weeks, or even months, many people on the leadership team quickly get lost in the weeds of details. They want to know how the change specifically will affect them. The leader's task is to continually bring the focus back to the need and the mission—the bigger picture. The process of discussion and planning will eventually answer the tactical questions, but as we've seen, it's a big mistake to jump too quickly to tactics and forget the larger, strategic vision to meet compelling needs.

Recasting a new vision is usually more challenging than casting the original one. The disappointment is a harsh reality, but it doesn't help to focus on the past. A fresh picture of the future is needed. The leader must deconstruct the new vision, in a dozen ways, describing what fulfilling the vision will mean to the people who are touched by it. A clear picture of the future helps people stay positive, and it soothes their recurring anxieties.

At the same time, the leader needs to be honest about the cost and the loss. All change involves loss, so acknowledging the losses before they happen gives the leader credibility in the eyes of his or her team. The leader patiently explains how changes in the systems and the organizational structure will affect each person, giving clarity and offering hope that the change will be worth it.

ANTICIPATING CHAOS

When Roosevelt made his commitment to complete the canal across Panama, he didn't resolve existing chaos; instead, he created plenty of it! Suddenly diplomats and engineers faced problems that had been dormant for a decade. His new vision created problems before solving any. In the same way, when we get a refreshed vision for our organizations, we multiply disruptions, at least at the beginning. If we anticipate them, we'll have the opportunity to prepare our people to handle them.

Irish organizational behavior

> When we get a refreshed vision for our organizations, we multiply disruptions, at least at the beginning.

expert Charles Handy popularized a concept about the growth and declines of business organizations, which he illustrated using a Sigmoid Curve. Handy's diagram shows how leaders can recognize and respond to signs of potential or actual decline. His chart begins simply by showing growth at Point A but stagnation and decline at Point B.[5]

Surprisingly, Handy concluded that Point A—not Point B—is the danger point. When organizations are growing and thriving, many leaders assume they'll continue to see remarkable growth into the foreseeable future.

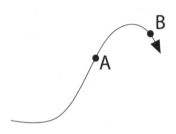

They often become complacent and over-confident, and they begin to coast instead of driving forward. They don't realize they're missing the opportunity to capitalize on the momentum they've generated.

Perceptive leaders predict the need to make changes *before* the decline occurs. Those who wait too long lose the momentum needed to make the changes more easily, but at Point A few people in the organization see the need for change. To most people, nothing is wrong; nothing needs to be fixed. The leader's task at that point is to explain that momentum will erode if they don't use it to catapult to the next level of growth. The leader injects a sense of urgency when most people only want to relax and enjoy success.

At this point in the organization's growth, the urgency of the leader may seem odd, and in fact, some may wonder if he's lost his mind. He's creating chaos when others assume all their efforts have effectively avoided it. But again, if the leader waits until everyone sees the need for change at Point B, it's far harder to recapture momentum and turn the ship around.

When leaders institute change at Point A by presenting a fresh vision of the future, they launch another cycle of growth. The leaders' urgency, hope, and bigger calling are combined with their followers' confusion, lethargy, and doubt. The time between the fresh vision at Point A and the new wave of momentum at B—often two years—is a Period of Chaos.

The first time a leader anticipates the need for a new vision at Point A and creates change can be the most trying time in his or her career. However, success breeds confidence. In the future, times of growth are interpreted as opportunities to launch the organization toward even more visionary goals, and the cycle repeats itself again and again.

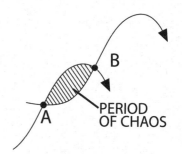

This repeating cycle of continuous change only happens when leaders are continually perceptive and continuously communicate a sense of urgency.[6] Many pastors, and some business leaders, value peace above all else. Chaos makes them uncomfortable, and creating chaos is unthinkable! These leaders need to step back and realize the cost when they value peace more than they do the opportunity for a surge in growth.

The apostle Paul advised the Christians in Rome to live in peace if at all possible (Rom. 12:18), but as Luke described Paul's life in Acts, we see him creating chaos in almost every city where he traveled. That's the double-edged knife of a leader: help people live in peace, but stir up enough chaos to make change happen. Real leaders see opportunities, they see potential in people, and they see the possibilities for their organizations to make a difference. Creating chaos may not seem natural to some leaders, but it's essential for all of us if we want to have a profound impact, if we want to be leaders and not caretakers.

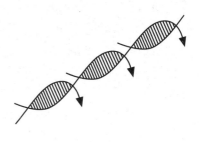

I often ask leaders several questions about change:

- In the last three to five years, when did your organization experience significant momentum?
- What created the forward movement?
- How did you respond when you had momentum? Did you capitalize on it, or did you let it drift away?
- If you let it drift, what could you have done differently to capture the momentum?

- How are you cultivating continuous perception and a continuous sense of urgency?
- Would people on your leadership team say you're always on alert, always optimistic, and always passionate about the next phase of growth? Explain your answer.

Chaos and conflict aren't the end of the world. They may signal genuine problems in an organization, but they may also be the inevitable friction between people who are passionate about moving toward a vision. If the organization is forward-focused, then conflict increases as change accelerates. Of course, it is best handled by diplomacy, negotiation, and building bridges. In a positive, can-do environment, leaders can model and teach the skills of constructively resolving conflict.

> That's the double-edged knife of a leader: help people live in peace, but stir up enough chaos to make change happen.

When I teach teams to use conflict constructively, I explain that conflict can be a big PLUS. They need to *Pause* to focus on the situation and the person without being distracted. Then they should *Listen* carefully, paraphrasing the other person's points. Ask questions and take time to *Understand* the other's position and then validate the person's feelings. Then *Solve* the problem together as a team, or if only one is responsible for the decision, at least the other person feels understood even if he or she disagrees.

- Pause
- Listen
- Understand
- Solve

No one ever accused Theodore Roosevelt of being passive and complacent. Every molecule, every word, and every action screamed, "We have to make this happen now!" He passionately believed he was destined to accomplish great things. This confidence propelled him to attempt great things and gather the very best people around him to get the job done. As I meet with top leaders around the world, some of them are like Roosevelt. They have two qualities that set them apart: they have an inner fire that burns with enormous energy, and they have an inner gyroscope that gives them direction. They pursue great things—in their businesses, in their churches, and in their nonprofit organizations—and they generate energy in the people around them. They fail plenty of times, but nothing holds them back from getting up and trying again.

WATERSHED

Let's be honest. Point A has the potential to be a turning point, a watershed moment for the leader and the organization, but many leaders miss it for different reasons. They may bask in the glow of success at Point A and enjoy the affirmation they receive from the many people who tell them, "Well done!" Or they may suffer from willful blindness; the opportunity for growth is right in front of them, but they close their eyes to it because it will require more effort, generate more change, and create more conflict than sitting back and looking at the fruit of previous labors. The period of chaos between Points A and B necessarily requires hard decisions about people they love who have served faithfully—or perhaps obstinate people who threaten to blow up if they are reassigned or released.

Another limiting factor is that many leaders are so busy they don't have enough margin to step away, think, talk to a mentor, pray, and dream of bigger things. Their plate is full and overflowing. They're already tired, and they can't imagine adding chaos to the mix! A significant effort to move forward necessarily involves assessing and updating both systems and structures—a daunting task even for those who have margin in their lives. They may have a fresh vision, but the cost of implementing it is just too high. In the next paragraphs, I'll explain practical ways to address these limiting factors.

Tenacity, patience, persistence, and attention to detail are essential at that crucial moment when leaders find themselves at Point A. When leaders make their plans to capture the momentum at Point A, some feel paralyzed by fears of the unknown. I encourage them to break the plan into its component parts. Then, for each part I ask, "What's the worst that can happen?" When they identify the worst, they understand they can handle it, so they feel free to dive in without reservations. The sequence is simple and profound: they deconstruct their plans into segments, consider the worst possible outcomes, and then work back to produce excellent and specific plans.

Many leaders who took steps to inject a renewed vision into their organizations have said, "Sam, I don't know what happened, but it didn't work." When I asked more pointed questions I realized, and I hope I helped them realize, they had tried to fulfill a new vision using their old systems and structures. If the vision is limited, then that may be workable, but if it's grand, it's not the idea's fault that it failed. The hope for more size and speed required the revamping of the way things work (the systems) and the way people work (the structure). *Bigger* and *faster* necessitate better *how* and *who*.

ASKING THE RIGHT QUESTIONS

All of us get up each day with two invaluable commodities: assumptions about the way life works and a range of experiences, from elation to crushing disappointments. We may not, however, come with the training to ask the most pertinent questions about our past, present, and future. Good questions focus our thinking and expand the possibilities. Many people—including many leaders— simply react to situations and people all day every day without doing the crucial work of thinking clearly. Education pioneer John Dewey reportedly observed, "We don't learn from experience; we learn by reflecting on experience."[7]

As I thought about my own thinking habits and patterns, I jotted down some questions leaders might consider:

> *Bigger* and *faster*
> necessitate better
> *how* and *who*.

- What are your foundational assumptions about God, about yourself, and about life? (These aren't just what you *say* you believe, but what you *truly* believe.)

> Good questions focus our thinking and expand the possibilities.

- How were those assumptions formed? Who or what has influenced you most powerfully?
- What process do you use in thinking? How effective is your process?
- How do you gather information?
- In any difficult situation, what are your most common questions?
- What is your default setting? In other words, in hard times, what thought patterns do you revert to?
- Who is the first person you think of when you need help with a problem?
- Who makes you think more deeply? How much time do you spend with that person?
- What concepts are you invested in learning more about?
- What do you need to unlearn?
- Whose thinking frustrates or infuriates you?
- Whose perspective brings you comfort, joy, and inspiration?
- Who knows what you think about yourself, God, those closest to you, and life?
- If you were completely open and vulnerable, what would you say and to whom?
- What can you do to improve your thinking skills?

RECHARGE

Some people have come to this point in the chapter and want to shout, "How can you tell me to take more time to think more deeply and clearly? I barely found time to read this far in your book!" I understand. One of the most common struggles of leaders is exhaustion—not just physical exhaustion, but mental, spiritual, emotional, and relational exhaustion. They're running on empty. I've been there too. It's difficult to lead with urgency, creativity, and enthusiasm if you're dead tired. For those in this condition, let me offer a few suggestions.

Find Friends and Mentors

A friend is your confidant and cheerleader, but a mentor is a coach who tells you things you may not want to hear. I think we all need a few friends and a mentor. With both, we need to be vulnerable. If we hold back the truth, we won't get the feedback and support we need. Psychologist Brené Brown has written about finding the inner strength to be honest. In *Daring Greatly* she wrote, "Courage starts with showing up and letting ourselves be seen. . . . Vulnerability sounds like truth and feels like courage. Truth and courage aren't always comfortable, but they're never weakness."[8]

> It's difficult to lead with urgency, creativity, and enthusiasm if you're dead tired.

Rediscover What You Love to Do

Leaders can drift. The pressures of the job, the need to pick up the pieces from team members who don't do their work well enough, and the multiplied stresses of leading an organization can consume our time and attention. Before long we're doing a lot of things we don't love to do, and we do far too little of the things that give us joy and energy. We need to regularly stop and analyze what we do each day and each week. If we're chronically frustrated, we may be feeling too much responsibility for things we don't do particularly well. We can't create a job that's 100 percent enjoyable, but for many of us, the percentage needs to be much higher than it is.

Celebrate Small Wins

Gratitude is a gift to God, a gift to those around us, and in truth, a gift to ourselves. When we notice the myriad of things that go right, the many people who do good work, and the many blessings of God, we breathe a sigh of relief and celebrate a little bit. Thankfulness is an essential leadership strength, and it is water for our thirsty souls.

Create More Time to Dream

If you don't build time to dream into your schedule, you'll always be operating on last year's hopes and vision. Dreams don't just happen. We need to carve out time and space so we can imagine what God might want to do, and as we spend time in his presence, we can listen.

IS IT WORTH IT?

Theodore Roosevelt had a renewed vision for a canal across Panama. To make that happen, he inspired a revolution. He created chaos to accomplish his goal. Every leader should ask, "Is it worth all the trouble?" The latest available figures show that 70 percent of the trade to and from the United States flows through the canal.[9] Without this artery between the oceans, all that cargo would have to travel much farther and cost significantly more. In addition, the US military relies on the canal to quickly move ships, service members, and material to trouble spots around the world.

The creation of the canal, as we'll see, was enormously expensive, but today every person in our country and many people across the world benefit from its existence. In the same way, leaders create chaos as they chart an even higher path from the success of Point A. They can choose to relax and enjoy their success, but sooner or later their organizations will stagnate and decline. Or they can pay the price of a new vision. The cost may be high, but they'll soon conclude it's worth it.

In the next chapter, we'll begin to see how Roosevelt's bold vision began to take shape. The first American chief engineer struggled as much as his French predecessors, but his replacement knew the importance of first creating excellent and effective systems that could get the maximum work out of the structure of engineers and workers.

THINK ABOUT THIS

Reflect on these questions and discuss them with your team:

1. Where is your organization on the Sigmoid Curve? How can you tell?
2. Answer the questions I often ask leaders about change:
   - In the last ten to fifteen years, when did your organization experience significant momentum?
   - What created the forward movement?
   - How did you respond when you had momentum? Did you capitalize on it, or did you let it drift away?
   - If you let it drift, what would you have done differently to capture the momentum?
   - How are you cultivating continuous perception and a continuous sense of urgency?
   - Would people on your leadership team say you're always on alert, always optimistic, and always passionate about the next phase of growth? Explain your answer.
3. When you come to the watershed moment at Point A, what are the obstacles you face—personally and organizationally? How will you overcome them?
4. Which of the suggestions in the "Recharge" section of the chapter do you need to apply? What steps will you take for each one?
5. What is the next practical step you'll make to take advantage of success in your organization? What will be the cost? What will be the benefits?

Remember: The size and speed of an organization are controlled by its systems and structures.

CHAPTER 4

HOW DO YOU CRAFT THE RIGHT PLAN?

For decades, several countries considered different routes across Central America. In the 1880s, the United States surveyed a path across Nicaragua using the vast expanse of Lake Nicaragua for much of the journey. However, concerns about volcanic activity and the elevation of the lake stopped the plans. US engineers considered a canal across the waist of Mexico, but the distance was too great. A route across Panama

Drills at Work
LIBRARY OF CONGRESS

at Darién, east of the present canal, had good harbors on both coasts, but the distance across the isthmus was significantly longer. Engineers also rejected yet another path farther east at the end of the isthmus at the Gulf of Urabá because a survey showed it would be much too expensive.

As American engineers considered different routes in 1902, the Nicaraguan plan still seemed viable. The Nicaraguan canal would need eight locks; the Panamanian canal would have six, including an extra one to account for the higher tides on the Pacific side. At a meeting to make a final decision on the route, a fierce debate between the existing French plan and one in Nicaragua raged for two weeks, but the Panama plan won a close vote, 42–34.

The French had already poured mountains of money, time, and effort into a route across Panama near the Chagres River. President Roosevelt tried to negotiate a treaty with the government of Colombia, but the Colombians were unwilling to give up control of the Canal Zone. Roosevelt's diplomats and the navy supported an almost bloodless revolution to separate the province of Panama from Colombia. Only about two weeks later, on November 18, 1903, the fledgling Panamanian government signed the Hay–Bunau-Varilla Treaty, ceding control of the ten-mile-wide Panama Canal Zone to the United States for $10 million and a $250 thousand annual annuity. The people of Colombia despised Theodore Roosevelt for his interference and the wound to their national pride. The people of America were just beginning to realize their president was a man of remarkable foresight and courage.

On the isthmus, the Americans were finally in the driver's seat. They had a treaty and control of the land, but they also had an abundance of outdated, rusting equipment and dilapidated buildings left over from the French. The existing systems and structure appeared to be an unmitigated disaster. The jungle environment caused wood to rot and metal to rust, and there appeared to be virtually no facilities for the enormous number of workers who would be required, first to build new systems, and then to use these systems to build the canal.

The big idea of completing the canal across Panama was very clear, but the plan to accomplish it was still up in the air. The first task was to catalog every asset that existed in the Canal Zone. While dredges three times as big as anything the French had used were being built in the United States, workers implemented a card index system to identify the existence and usefulness of everything they saw. Surprisingly, they found some buildings, trains, dredges, and other equipment were still usable.

The first chief engineer was John Findley Wallace. He launched into the daunting work, but he soon experienced the frustrations of having to deal with delays caused by Congress, which tried to micromanage the project from thousands of miles away. The men hired to work were not exactly the cream of the crop. After they arrived, Wallace discovered that "experienced track hands" he counted on to haul equipment by rail had never worked on a railroad. Others came to Panama because they had been blacklisted in America. They had ruined their reputations—and limited their career opportunities—through alcoholism and drifting from job to job. The recruits had been promised nice accommodations, but they suffered in unfinished, cramped quarters with poor food and backbreaking work.

Wallace was soon overwhelmed. He resigned and was replaced by John Frank Stevens, who arrived in January 1905. Stevens immediately realized the infrastructure, the systems, had to be upgraded in every area: the railroad, housing, sanitation, and equipment. Only then could he recruit—and keep—the thousands of workers required to complete the job.

Even at this point, two years after the Americans took over the canal, the plans hadn't been finalized. Though the French had given up on the sea-level route across the isthmus, the dream of a Suez-type canal wouldn't die. When Stevens arrived, he assumed he would be building a canal without locks. The biggest obstacle was the hills of Culebra. One creative proposal was to use powerful blasts of water, a technique typically used in hydraulic mining, to wash the hills into the ocean. Another equally fantastic idea was to use compressed air to blow up rocks and drive the pieces into the sea.

Stevens created a remarkable system of trains to serve as a conveyor belt, carrying dirt and rock from steam shovels to the coasts or to dam sites. The double tracks kept trains moving continuously, making the system far more effective than anyone had seen before. Building the infrastructure and the tracks took the entire year. In early 1906, Stevens was ready to resume excavation at Culebra. It had been more than two years since the treaty was signed, but Stevens knew he needed to do the hard, thankless, and seemingly ineffective work of creating better systems before they could begin digging again.

Stevens had a clear vision of both the goal and the cost to achieve it. He wrote his observations about the nine miles of excavation at Culebra, the greatest challenge to the engineers:

> Yet we must reflect that at best, even with the backing and sentiment and finances of the most powerful nation on earth, that we are contending with Nature's forces, and that while our wishes and ambition are of great assistance in a work of this magnitude, neither the inspiration of genius nor our optimism will build this canal. Nothing but dogged determination and steady, persistent, intelligent work will ever accomplish the result; and when we speak of a hundred million yards of a single cut not to exceed nine miles in length, we are facing a proposition greater than was ever undertaken in the engineering history of the world.[1]

Historian David McCullough painted a picture of Stevens: "Day after day he trudged about among the men and machines, asking questions, observing, smoking cigars like Grant at the [Battle of the] Wilderness, as a reporter noted. The men called him 'Big Smoke.'"[2]

Later that year Stevens reported to Congress that the time to complete a canal with locks was estimated to be nine years, finishing in 1914. The time needed to complete a sea-level canal would be at least eighteen years, not completed until 1924. The vote in Congress was very close, but they realized speed was essential. It would be a lock canal after all. Finalizing the plan had taken dozens of detailed surveys, decades of trial and error, and the best minds in the field of engineering, but now all the resources could be focused on the plan and the goal.

YOUR FILTER

All of us want to be as objective as possible as we analyze data and make plans, but we should realize we have filters: predispositions that shape our thinking, screening out or minimizing some facts and giving more weight to others. De Lesseps and many of the American engineers desperately wanted to dig a canal like the Suez—a clean, simple, fast, sea-level path between the oceans. In extensive surveys and analysis by different commissions, many of the engineers and political leaders kept leaning toward this solution, even in the face of mounting evidence that it was impractical. Millions of dollars were wasted as the debate raged for decades. They analyzed the realities in Panama by using their own distorted filters.

As leaders, we should realize our filters exist. Even our strongest commitment to objectivity has at least tinges of subjectivity. We are influenced by who presents the data, how it's presented, and who on our team takes sides for or against the recommendation based on the data. These factors—and many others, including our current stress levels, team dynamics, how much sleep we got last night, and how quickly we want to make this decision—affect how we interpret information and craft plans. We never receive input and analysis in an objective bubble; we always have predispositions that shape our receptivity and our ability to process information. If we understand our existing leanings, we can at least ask a question or two to get more objective input.

PLANNING AND PREPARATION

A big vision usually starts with the primary leader, like Roosevelt's bold commitment to succeed where the French had failed. A compelling vision, though, remains only an inspiring strategic concept until the leader involves competent people in the tactical planning to make it happen. The leader often has a good idea of the what, but he usually doesn't have a good grasp of when, where, who, how, and how much. The planning phase must be pushed down to the level where many skilled, passionate, creative people give their best efforts to craft a comprehensive plan. But even then, it's always flexible enough to be changed when new challenges and opportunities present themselves. The leader articulates the need and the big idea of meeting the need, but he enlists others to create plans to

> As leaders, we should realize our filters exist.

identify the size and the speed, and then to create the systems and structures to achieve those goals.

Leaders may ask too quickly: "Is this big idea realistic?" This question needs to be asked at the tactical level. If it's asked too soon, it short-circuits the essential process of dreaming big dreams. By their nature, big dreams don't seem realistic at all! But on the other side, if a vision isn't keeping a leader up at night, it's not big enough. A dream should be so challenging that it inflames the leader's deepest passions and demands the best ideas.

> By their nature, big dreams don't seem realistic at all!

To begin the planning process, carefully choose a team of wise, optimistic, experienced, creative people. The members should have diverse perspectives—not so radical that their demands will burn the house down, but different enough to produce sparks that will ignite the best discussions. They need to be forthright about both the obstacles and the possible solutions. I want people who feel the freedom to poke holes in others' ideas but who can also affirm good ideas when other people come up with them. I also want people who know how to implement the plans we craft. They can't just be dreamers; they also need to be doers.

When I consult with leaders about planning, I suggest the same four elements I use with my team:

1. In the first meeting at the beginning of the planning process, I share the big idea, and I tell them we're going to brainstorm to begin to shape it. We aren't going to make any decisions. I invite the members of the team to engage in blue-sky thinking: no limits, nothing off the table, and no criticism of anyone's wild ideas. In this meeting, our goal isn't to draft plans. The goal is only to dream—and to dream big dreams.

   A lot of leaders feel the pressure to be "the decider" much too early in the process, but their primary job isn't to be the decider at all. Their task is to cast a big vision and invite the team to be part of shaping the dream almost from the beginning. When members of the team catch fire, their contributions will be flaming hot with creative ideas, clear plans, and a commitment to follow through with every detail.

2. A few days later, the team meets again. The leader tells them, "Now that you've had some time to think about the big idea, what are your thoughts about how this might happen?"

    On our team, we still don't make any decisions in this meeting. We're beginning to pour cement, but it's still quite wet. In this conversation, the issues of sustainability and scalability begin to take shape.

3. Perhaps a week later, we have our third meeting. In the days between meetings, the team members have met informally many times to discuss their ideas and potential plans. These sidebar conversations stimulate creativity, but they also begin to shape real plans and coordination. In the third meeting, however, we aren't planning yet. We're clarifying definitions, and we're putting boundaries around what fulfilling the vision will be and won't be. We don't establish the exact systems and structures; we only make sure we identify the needs that must be met to accomplish the vision. We know we'll need to address financial and technical issues, but we haven't defined any roles to meet those needs.

    In the third meeting, leaders are in no hurry to come up with a detailed plan to present to the board, the investors, or anyone else. Haste stops the dreaming process, limits creative thinking, and sends the wrong message to the team that the real goal is having a final plan neatly copied and put in a binder.

4. The next several team meetings are designed to create the strategic and tactical plans. By this time, every person on the team has bought into the vision and contributed to the definition of how fulfilling it will benefit the community and the organization. Now it's time to craft the strategic plans to define the size and speed and then drill down to create the tactical plans to define the specifics of the systems and structures.

This process works in any organization. For example, the owner of a real estate company may have a meeting with the marketing and sales team to tell them, "I've been thinking. We have an opportunity to expand into a part of the market where we haven't done much. I want to have a series of planning meetings with you to get your input and come up with a workable plan. First, I want us to dream together. We don't need to make any plans or decisions yet. Let's just let our imaginations go. What do we offer that the other companies don't? How can we capture this market and really make a difference?" In the first meeting, they're dreaming together.

In the second meeting, a few days later, the owner goes around the table and asks each person, "What are your thoughts about the big idea?" Almost always, several members of the team will come up with insights the owner never imagined. They leave this meeting with the promise to come back again to make more progress. The team realizes this idea is too big to hurry through.

Between meetings, team members talk to each other to consider ideas and see what others think. If the vision is big enough, they realize everyone will benefit—their clients, their company, and themselves.

In the third conversation around the table, the ideas begin to gel even more. The owner may ask, "What will make us different? What can we do that will set us apart?" These questions are similar to ones asked in the first meeting, but now the answers are sharper and clearer than before. Gradually the team realizes their best efforts should be given to the residential market, with homes between $300,000 and $700,000. That's the sweet spot, where their company can best serve their community.

The next set of meetings is designed to define how big the plans need to be, how fast the team can reach their goal, the internal systems that need to be updated or created to achieve it, the responsibilities for each member of the team, and perhaps the need to recruit a few new people to make it all happen. The team can then create budgets and marketing plans, and they can instruct their people how to handle calls inside and outside the parameters of their market focus. As always, the size and speed are determined by the systems and structure.

Even if the owner had this exact outcome in mind before beginning this series of meetings, the brainstorming and planning process involved the team, brought out their best ideas, and gave them far more motivation to make it happen. And their input undoubtedly fine-tuned and improved the owner's original plans, no matter how good they were.

In this process, the leader's goal isn't to build consensus around his own ideas. Instead, he's mining the wisdom of his team to produce a much better plan and a much higher level of passion to accomplish it. It takes a little longer, but the benefits far outweigh the meager costs.

I've seen a team's lethargy—and sometimes real damage to the organizational culture—that occurs when leaders don't involve their teams in a creative process. For instance, a pastor may read an article about the latest great idea: small groups, multisite churches, leadership pipelines, a new kind of sound system, or whatever it may be. He or she announces the new initiative and then tells someone on the team, "Visit this church [or read this book or watch this video] and make this happen at our church." When this happens, there is no vision exchange, no creative involvement of the entire team, and very little buy-in, even from the person who is assigned to pull it off. The team member is just following orders.

> In this process, the leader's goal isn't to build consensus around his own ideas.

Projects handled in this way are dead before they begin. Any leader who wants to succeed should figure out a way to be better than this.

UNIQUE CONTRIBUTIONS

The creative process of involving the team often reveals that one member of the team is uniquely suited to take greater responsibility to fulfill the vision, or more likely, all the people on the team can play particular—and particularly important—roles. All builders aren't the same. People who build houses don't build bridges; people who build bridges don't build stadiums; people who build stadiums don't build shopping centers; people who build shopping centers don't build hospitals; and people who build hospitals don't build airports.

When I sit next to someone on a plane, I almost invariably ask, "What do you do for a living?" If the person says, "I'm a builder," I ask, "Great. What do you build?" If he says, "Shopping centers," I then ask, "Wonderful. Where do you build them? I know the ones in cities are very different from those in the suburbs." The builder is often surprised that I've identified this distinction, and I then get a detailed review of the demographics, types of stores, parking specifications, and traffic flow of the centers he builds.

One of the problems I frequently encounter is that leaders haven't clearly identified the kinds of builders on their teams. They expect everybody to do everything. One or two may be in exactly the right spot to excel, but others may be like square pegs in round holes. It's not their fault they don't fit. They're usually trying as hard as they can. It's the leader's job to assess each person's specific talent as a builder and assign team members to roles where they can excel.

Too often leaders in businesses, churches, and nonprofit organizations walk into meetings and announce, "This is what I've decided we're going to build," or from a spiritual angle, "This is what I believe God wants us to build." When a leader jumps too soon from the dream to the plan, the people on the team don't have the opportunity to dream, and they don't feel affirmed in their unique contributions as builders.

PLANNING VS. PREPARATION

It's helpful to distinguish between planning and preparation. Planning is concrete; it answers the what, who, when, where, how, and how much. Preparation is usually intangible and answers the why questions. Leaders need to pursue the why of any endeavor: Why does the community need this project? Why would it be right for our organization and our team? Why am I motivated to accomplish it?

When our family takes a vacation, the trip itself is the what. The planning process assures that we'll get to the airport on time, take the best flights, stay in good places, and have tickets to the things we want to see. We prepare as a family by talking about the fun we'll have, why we're excited about going, and the memories we'll make. In the process, planning devolves into more specifics, and preparation evolves into greater anticipation.

> When a leader jumps too soon from the dream to the plan, the people on the team don't have the opportunity to dream, and they don't feel affirmed in their unique contributions as builders.

Most of the leaders I know excel in planning, but they are often deficient in preparation—for themselves, their teams, and their organizations.

SLOW DOWN AND LISTEN

I know plenty of leaders who are predisposed to insist on their own ideas without involving others in the planning process, but I also have the privilege of watching some collaborative leaders who continually inspire the people on their teams by taking time to involve them in every step from conception to completion. These leaders feel comfortable with ambiguity at the beginning. They know they'll get to the specifics soon enough, and if they take their time and ask for the best from each person, they'll almost certainly get an exceptional plan and the passionate commitment of their remarkable people. When their people feel valued, they gladly share innovative ideas, wisdom, and experience. For these leaders, it's an investment of time and initial uncertainty that pays big dividends.

A longer process of planning requires a higher level of leadership skills. When leaders encourage team members to be creative, will some people chase rabbits and come up with totally off-the-wall ideas? Of course, but that's not a problem. Creativity always produces a fair share of irrelevant and unproductive ideas, but it also has the potential to generate the best ideas. The leader's task is to harness all that creativity, celebrate it, but

> A longer process of planning requires a higher level of leadership skills.

know when it's time to put the rabbit back in the cage so the team can focus on concepts that offer more promise.

The fact that the leader encourages this creativity, though, sends a message. It tells the team that each person's ideas are incredibly valuable. I believe team tension would be resolved in many cases if leaders learned to plan this way. Love covers a multitude of sins, and feeling valued covers a ton of tension.

What does this kind of inspiring leadership sound like? It has many expressions. For example, when a leader is working through an agenda in a team meeting and says, "I know we have some other important things on the list to cover today, but Jane, you just said something really important.

> Love covers a multitude of sins, and feeling valued covers a ton of tension.

Would you take a few minutes to unpack that thought for us? I think this might stimulate some ideas we, or at least I, haven't thought before." If the idea is significant, the leader may say, "That's really important, Jane. We don't have time to go deeper with it right now, but let's talk about it more at our next meet-

ing. Would you write up your thoughts in more detail and send them to us so we can talk about it then?" How do you think Jane feels at that moment? Do you think others look forward to sharing their best ideas with the team?

Creativity seldom appears in the middle of a carefully controlled agenda. It comes at the inspired edges when people feel free to share their ideas. In these open-minded moments, leaders invite people to consider, "What if —," "If we only could—," "Can you imagine—," and "Could it be possible—." For this level of inspiration to occur, leaders must be secure enough to value others' ideas as much as their own, they need to be perceptive enough to recognize when a team member's idea is worth adjusting the agenda to make room for it, and they need to be wise enough to welcome all creative ideas without losing control of the team.

I think it's a good rule in all important relationships—with a spouse, children, a board, friends, and a team—to regularly say, "Tell me more about that." If we aren't making this statement at least two or three times a week, we aren't paying enough attention to the people God has put in our lives. This simple statement and the time to listen take only a few minutes, but it can radically change the tone of a relationship, the mood of a team, and the culture of an organization.

One of the most common complaints I hear from senior leaders is that they're tired. They groan as they tell me, "I'm exhausted, drained, burned-out. All the good ideas for our organization have to come from me." They're complaining about the people on their teams, but they've pointed their finger at the wrong problem.

At some later time, I say to them, "So, it seems you have doers around the table, not thinkers."

Their eyes widen, and they say, "Yes, that's it!"

I then ask, "How do you suppose that happened?"

In the subsequent conversation, I help them realize their people have stopped thinking and being creative because the leader has done all the thinking and creating for a long time. When people first joined the team, they were energetic and innovative. They wanted to contribute, and they were excited about their roles. Over many months when their ideas weren't affirmed (or even heard), they became silent robots.

Maybe they asked questions that were perceived as threats, or maybe they got buried in the red tape of meaningless bureaucracy. After a while, they concluded that all the leader wants from them is to sit, take notes, and follow directions. They could still contribute as gifted thinkers, but their creativity isn't being cultivated, nourished, valued, and used.

> Creativity seldom appears in the middle of a carefully controlled agenda.

Usually the leaders with whom I have this frank conversation realize they've contributed to the problem. In fact, in every meeting, they've reinforced the power differential: the leader has all the ideas, and the people on the team are only tools to carry them out.

Do you go into meetings believing there's a remote possibility the people on your team might have a better idea than yours? Do you go into meetings thinking that the people on your team might have a clearer and better concept of the outcome of a project than you dreamed possible? Are you genuinely glad when someone on your team has a creative idea? Are you and your ideas improvable? These are the unspoken questions—and the positive answers are the inherent assumptions—of collaborative leaders.

Most leaders I know would say they are collaborative, but in meetings they are drivers not passengers. They walk into each meeting with a clear outcome in mind, and nothing is going to keep them from accomplishing their goal. I'm not saying they shouldn't be drivers; that's an important part of their role. But I'm strongly suggesting they need to carve out times and find ways to be passengers more often.

I've described how they can be passengers in a four-part planning process, but they also need to practice being passengers in every meeting at least some of the time. Some are so goal driven and such strong type-A personalities that this will be a struggle. I'd tell them: Make it a goal to see yourself as a passenger in parts of every meeting and in all of some meetings. And practice saying, "Tell me more about that" once a day until it becomes a habit.

I've often walked into meetings and said something like, "I have an idea. I think it's a *good* idea, but it's far from a *great* idea. I need your help to expand it, shape it up, and make sense of it. Will you help me?" I share my idea, and then I sit back and say, "Okay, give me your thoughts on how we can make it better." Quite often I come out of that meeting with something far better than—and sometimes totally different from—my original idea.

PLANNING AND CHARACTER

The process of analysis, vision casting, strategic planning, and tactical assignments doesn't happen only on a whiteboard with nice boxes and lines. It's a thoroughly human endeavor, and as we've seen, the leader's primary role is to bring out the best in his or her team so their creativity and passion produces not only a brilliant plan but also a phenomenal outcome. The atmosphere the leader creates is the air the team breathes—the more life-giving oxygen, the better.

Insecure leaders feel the need to have all the answers, and they feel threatened when others don't instantly buy into them or have better answers. But strong, secure leaders realize their chief task is to provide security for those around them. Only then will those people have the confidence to bring their best to every meeting, conversation, project, and task.

The planning process begins with blue-sky dreaming, but at some point leaders need to blend visionary optimism with steely-eyed realism. When leaders engage in too much "happy talk," their followers may be inspired at first but soon realize their leaders aren't living in the real world. Famous

> Strong, secure leaders realize their chief task is to provide security for those around them.

newsman Edward R. Murrow explained that honesty is essential if leaders want to move hearts: "To be persuasive we must be believable; to be believable we must be credible; to be credible we must be truthful."[3]

Persuading hearts almost always takes longer than giving orders and demanding instant compliance. Of course, some are unwilling to be persuaded. After giving them enough time to show their colors, we need to release them. But most people genuinely want to get on board. Some just need a little more information and coaxing than others.

When Dwight Eisenhower led the Allied forces in the invasion of Europe on D-Day, he not only had to deal with generals like Omar Bradley, who were eager to follow orders, but he also had to find a way to lead men like George Patton and Bernard Montgomery, who were often headstrong and defiant. Eisenhower later reflected, "I would rather try to persuade a man to go along, because once I have persuaded him he will stick. If I scare him, he will stay just as long as he is scared, and then he is gone."[4]

WHAT YOU MEASURE

Our people notice what we value, and what we value we always find a way to measure. In other words, we measure what matters. In planning, we obviously are in the process of creating a new measuring stick, one with an expanded size achieved at greater speed. The process of establishing those benchmarks takes time, but once we have them, they're easy to notice and they clearly gauge our progress. But those aren't the only things we measure, because those aren't the only things we value.

We also devote energy to measure the effectiveness of our systems and structures because those are the vehicles that will get us to our goals. For instance, one of the most important, but often the most overlooked, items to measure in a church is the percentage of attenders who are actively involved as volunteers. But even then, our people are looking to us to see if we value the intangibles of their ideas and their passion. If we focus only on numbers—very important numbers, no doubt, but still numbers—we run the risk of sending the wrong message to our people.

Look beyond the obvious things we measure: attendance, buildings, and cash. Begin to measure the times you say, "Tell me more about that," the times your staff members are excited about sharing new ideas, the rabbits you're willing to chase in a staff meeting, and the laughter and tears that are always products of authentic, vulnerable relationships.

The planning process at the Panama Canal took years and an enormous amount of analysis before John Stevens and his team of engineers decided to build a canal with locks instead of trying to dig enough for a sea-level route. They finally knew the most important feature of their plan, but now they had to construct the canal so the new, larger cargo ships could navigate it. Their work was just beginning.

THINK ABOUT THIS

Reflect on these questions and discuss them with your team:

1. What are some ways you can identify your predispositions that shape your analysis and your plans? Is it even important to notice them? Why or why not?

2. As you evaluate the four-part planning process outlined in this chapter, which parts do you already do well? What needs some improvement?

3. How would you describe the different kinds of "builders" on your team? How can you give them assignments that fit their unique talents?

4. Sometime today, stop in the middle of a conversation when someone has said something important and say, "Tell me more about that." What difference do you think this simple invitation will make to that person? And to your relationship?

5. What do you think you measure? What do your people think you measure? Are any changes needed?

Remember: The size and speed of an organization are controlled by its systems and structures.

CHAPTER 5

WHAT'S IN YOUR SUITCASE?

If we stand at the shore of a ship channel in any major port and look at the enormous vessels that are at the docks or in the waterway, we may be tempted to think this snapshot shows us how ships have always been built. But that's not the case. Shipbuilding is a continuous revolution. Designers are always trying to build crafts bigger and faster than before—size and speed. When John Stevens and his team of engineers began designing the locks for the Panama Canal, shipbuilding was going through a rapid transformation. Only a few decades before,

Culebra Cut

steam propulsion was introduced to the seas, and some ships were still under sail. By the turn of the twentieth century, the power generated by increasingly efficient engines—widely using coal and soon oil—would continue to revolutionize shipping.

The designers at the canal knew they were in the active flow of maritime history, so they had to anticipate the size of ships in the foreseeable future. As they were drafting their blueprints, they had to build locks to fit ships larger than existing cargo ships, battleships, and passenger steamers. At a meeting of the Institution of Naval Architects in 1907, a paper was presented that showed cargo ships had increased in length from an average of 240 feet in 1870 to 320 feet in 1900. This represented an 11 percent growth in length each decade, and it showed no signs of slowing down.

In 1906, the British launched the HMS *Dreadnought*, the most formidable warship on the seas at 527 feet long and 82 feet wide. Passenger ships were even larger. In 1907 the Cunard Line launched the RMS *Lusitania*, which was sunk by a German submarine during World War I with the loss of many US citizens, a significant factor in bringing America into the war. This steamer was 790 feet long and 88 feet wide.

The size of all types of ships was growing rapidly, so the engineers needed to build the canal for the future, not the past or the present. They first drew plans for lock chambers 1,000 feet long and 95 feet wide, but they decided to widen the locks to 110 feet. That, they were sure, would accommodate ocean vessels in the canal for a very long time.

Their foresight, though, multiplied the difficulties of construction. They had to design and build three sets of locks on each side of the canal, and to increase the speed of travel they designed double locks in all six places—there would be two lanes of traffic, not one.

Much of the navigable route over the fifty miles of the canal would be through Gatun Lake, which was created by damming the Chagres River and controlling the flow during both dry and rainy seasons. But the locks on each end had to be stable, secure, and strong. The gates would be of colossal size and weight. They couldn't be anchored in dirt. Two thousand years earlier, the Romans had invented and perfected the use of concrete as a building material. Today many of the structures they built of this material attest to its durability. Concrete wasn't widely used in the West, however, even in the late nineteenth and early twentieth centuries.

Stevens selected three engineers to oversee the design and construction of the locks and gates: Lieutenant Colonel Harry Hodges, Edward Schildhauer, and Henry Goldmark. These men believed concrete was the key to the success of the canal. They tried different mixtures of sand, cement, and gravel until they found a formula they believed would serve their purposes. The results were spectacular. For four years, beginning in August 1909, they built forms and mixed and poured more than two million cubic yards of concrete to create the chambers that would hold the water supporting the ships in the locks.

Of all the engineering marvels at the canal, perhaps the most difficult to conceive and build were the gates to open and close each end of each set of locks. The largest was 82 feet high and weighed 662 tons. Each of them had to be opened and closed relatively quickly with a powerful electrical motor. Ably assisted by Schildhauer, Hodges was responsible for the construction of the gates. Some said the canal simply could not have been completed without his expertise.

The engineers used the power of water to generate electricity. It flowed through gigantic tunnels from the lake down toward the oceans, turning the blades of generators and producing enough electric power to open and close the huge gates and power the electric needs of the operation.

Stevens and his engineers had to anticipate the increasing size of ships that would use the canal in the coming decades, and shipbuilders around the world were watching them closely. Size limits, called Panamax specifications, were issued by the Panama Canal Commission in 1914, and soon shipyards designed and built ships that had the maximum capacity to go through the locks. These Panamax ships could be up to 965 feet long and 106 feet wide, leaving only 2 feet on each side of the 110-foot-wide locks.

If the designers had built the Panama Canal for existing ships, it would have been outdated within a few years. But they didn't; they designed it for the future.

ANTICIPATION

One of the most important traits of outstanding leaders—at all levels of organizations—is the ability to anticipate the opportunities and challenges of the future. More than ever, this trait is essential today. Why? Because our society is changing at warp speed. It hasn't always been this way. Historian

William Manchester observed that during the millennium of the Dark Ages, from the fall of Rome in the fifth century to the Reformation and the rise of nation-states in the sixteenth century, cultural progress was almost nonexistent. People lived in isolated hamlets, with no concept of time: they didn't even know the years they were born, lived, or died. They toiled according to the endless cycles of seasons. Manchester explained their isolation:

> There were no newspapers or magazines to inform the common people of great events; occasional pamphlets might reach them, but they were usually theological and, like the Bible, were always published in Latin, a language they no longer understood. . . . [They had no expectation that] they should be informed about great events, let alone have any voice in them. Their anonymity approached the absolute. So did their mute acceptance of it.[1]

Late in the fifteenth century, Gutenberg's printing press ushered in a new world of literacy, and in a few short decades, many people throughout Europe had literature written and printed in their own languages. Exploration and travel opened new horizons, communication improved vastly, and Western civilization as we know it began to take shape. The next leap forward occurred in the eighteenth century with the Industrial Revolution. Marvelous new machines produced goods and raised the standard of living for the vast majority of people. Steam power, fueled by coal and oil, caused the rapid expansion of economies, but the magnificent machines of commerce could easily be converted into weapons of indescribable carnage. In the twentieth century, two world wars, a cataclysmic depression, and political revolutions in

One of the most important traits of outstanding leaders is the ability to anticipate the opportunities and challenges of the future.

two of the world's great nations led to the deaths of as many as two hundred million people.

At the end of the Second World War, a fledgling version of the modern computer was invented, and the world hasn't looked back since. Computing power has made the information age a life-altering reality for almost every person on the planet. The phones we carry in our pockets have far more capability than the computer aboard the spacecraft that landed on the moon in July 1969. Computers have changed how we work, how we communicate, how we're entertained, how we shop, and now, even the way we travel in our cars. And all of this has happened in the relative blink of a historical eye.

Cultural change, though, isn't limited to technology. Rapid and sweeping advances are changing virtually every part of our lives. The advances have made information more accessible and convenient, but some see hidden dangers. In his insightful book *Margin*, Dr. Richard Swenson observed:

> Future history books will need to use a different vocabulary to describe contemporary phenomena, and prominent among these words will be "exponential," "limits," "thresholds," and "overload." . . . Life, change, history—all are unfolding exponentially. . . . Many people, however, are trapped in a linear paradigm, a mind-set that can only see straight ahead. While they understand qualitative changes, they have failed to comprehend the quantitative nature of "future shock."[2]

Leaders desperately need to get in front of the wave—for the sake of their own sanity so they aren't overwhelmed, as well as for the future of their organizations. Those who are paying attention ask, "Where is all this going so fast?" "How does this affect our organization?" "How do we need to re-create our systems and structures to prepare for what's coming?" and "What do we need to do to get in front of all this?"

We can cultivate the ability to anticipate the needs of the future. Leaders need to look into the future to recognize trends in demographics, interests, and receptivity to their message and products. For example, in an article in the *Atlantic*, Robert P. Jones reviewed the increasing gap in spiritual

> Leaders desperately need to get in front of the wave—for the sake of their own sanity so they aren't overwhelmed, as well as for the future of their organizations.

interest between older and younger Americans. Among Boomers sixty-five and older, only 11 percent claim "no religious affiliation," commonly known as "nones." But for young adults eighteen to twenty-nine, the nones represent 34 percent. Jones concluded, "By 2051, if current trends continue, religiously unaffiliated Americans could comprise as large a percentage of the population as Protestants—which would have been unimaginable just a few decades ago."[3]

Jones and other commentators assert the church is losing a generation of young people. Why is this happening? In a rapidly changing and closely connected culture, the church is viewed as out of step with issues important to Millennials, such as immigration, racial justice, economic opportunity, health care, and the rights of those the church has traditionally considered misfits and outcasts—the kinds of causes the church championed for two thousand years.

The business world must anticipate needs and stay in front of changing demand for products and services; the church must anticipate the intangible social and spiritual expectations of people—especially young people—in our culture.

I have a picture of a giraffe in my office. It reminds me that this amazing creature sees farther out into the African savanna than any other land animal. It's not the most beautiful, and it's not the most graceful. It has a limited food source, and it can thrive only in a certain type of geography. To be honest, the giraffe looks as though it came from a Dr. Seuss book. From a distance, it can see hungry lions lurking in the tall grass or leopards in trees, and it can spot waterholes and trees full of nourishing leaves. All great leaders see *farther* than others, and they see challenges and opportunities *sooner* than others. I want to be that kind of leader.

When I hear leaders and their teams resist new ideas because "we've never done it this way before," I know they're stuck in the past—they're moles, not giraffes. If I hear them complain about all the limitations of people, space, money, and time, I know they're paralyzed in the present—they're turtles, not giraffes.

> All great leaders see *farther* than others, and they see challenges and opportunities *sooner* than others.

We need to take a long, hard look at our assumptions about the people we're trying to reach, whether in business, the church, or nonprofits. Are our assumptions antiquated or up-to-date? Does our language fit the current vernacular without being too trendy? Are our plans flexible and nimble? Do our products and messages attract a certain part of the audience but repel others—or leave them disinterested? Those who lead businesses like Apple and Amazon are giraffes. Similarly, some churches have rediscovered the heart of the gospel, the power of the mission, and the ability to connect these with a wide audience. The leaders of these churches are giraffes too.

TAKE A LOOK IN YOUR SUITCASE

Let me use a different metaphor to make a similar point. When I pack for a trip, I look at the weather report at my destination. If I'm going to Chicago in January, I pack very differently than if I'm going to San Antonio in August. Someone who opens my suitcase might not know my exact destination, but the contents would make it clear what conditions I anticipate.

If I unpack your organizational suitcase, what will I find? Are you packed for where your organization has been since the nineteenth century, are you packed for where you are today, or are you packed for your future?

In any suitcase we find the skills and vision of our leadership team. We dig down farther and pull out the systems. Are they the ones that have brought us this far and can take us no farther, or are they systems that can take us to the next level of growth? In your communication, how much time is spent analyzing the past? How much is spent focusing on the present? And how much is devoted to anticipating the future? In the church we have a rich and storied history we want to cherish, but we don't want to be captives of our history. The reason it's rich and storied is that bold men and women saw into the future and made dramatic decisions that changed the world.

I find too many leaders who don't even consider the weather report at their destination. They're too busy making their current systems and structures work to even think about the future beyond the coming weeks and months. Cultural analysis and the potential for sweeping change to capture the hearts of their audience don't even occur to them.

FUTURING

We all stand under the same sky, but our horizons are different. Some see a mile, but others see ten miles. I realize some leaders, especially many pastors, are wired to be *nurturers*. They're tender and compassionate, meeting the needs of hurting people every day. Other leaders are *futurers*, scanning the horizon like giraffes to look for lions to avoid or delicious leaves to eat. Both types of leaders can use their existing strengths, and both can develop new skills.

Compassionate leaders can learn to lengthen their necks to see farther into the future so they can direct their compassion even more effectively. Nurturers may develop the ability to see two miles into the future, but futurers see five miles, far over the horizon and beyond the vision of the antelope and other land-hugging animals. And futurers can learn to gently nudge their young in the right directions—to avoid being eaten and to find nourishment.

Whether you're wired as a nurturer or a futurer, I recommend every leader put together a "futuring team": a diverse group of men and women tasked with anticipating the demographics of the future. What will the school system look like? Where is economic growth happening, and where will it be stagnant? What ethnic groups are moving in, and which are moving out? Where do the CEOs of fast-food restaurants plan to expand? Which parts of the community will have predominantly older people? Which parts will attract younger people? Downtown neighborhoods are very different from the suburbs. Which are slated to grow?

Some of the people on the futuring team may have a clearer picture of the future than you do. Some youth pastors are much more in tune with the changing culture because they are vitally connected to the kids, volunteers, and young parents—on the cutting edge of communication, values, and expectations in society. In addition, the youth pastor has no hang-ups about using the latest technology. That's his world, so he stays on top of it.

> I recommend every leader put together a "futuring team."

Leaders of large organizations need to include two kinds of people in the planning process: the leaders of specialized divisions, (in churches—students, children, worship, small groups, etc.; and in companies—marketing, distribution, IT, manufacturing, etc.) and the most insightful people who are in touch with the culture. In small organizations, leaders can invite particularly astute employees or the sharpest volunteers.

The senior leader is a globalist and generalist. Those on the futuring team are usually specialists who have a vested interest in being giraffes to anticipate the needs in the future. We can look to this team for insights and innovative ideas. The members of the team can tell us what needs to be thrown out of our suitcase because those things won't be useful in our future.

As part of planning for the future, rebranding may be necessary. For instance, a famous fried-chicken fast-food chain has changed its name to eliminate "fried" because the word has a negative connotation in our increasingly health-conscious society. All organizations need to look at how their brand is perceived by those they hope to reach in the future.

The question we ask each person on the futuring team is, "If we were to pack our suitcase today to be ready for tomorrow, what do we need to throw out and what do we need to include?" Futuring leaders instinctively ask this question, and nurturing leaders can learn to ask it.

NO LIMITATIONS

I'm sure personality profiles and spiritual gifts inventories have helped countless people understand themselves and find a good fit in their organizations, but on balance, I'm afraid they do as much harm as good. When we define someone's personality or talents, we often confine him or her to act and serve in a narrow, constricted way.

If you use these tools for yourself and others, be sure to avoid the constrictions. No matter what your personality assessment and your gift mix may be, don't put yourself in a box. God can use you in ways that are far beyond any natural limitations. And don't use these instruments as excuses for lethargy.

God has made us wonderfully complex, and our lives are dynamic—we can grow and change in remarkable ways—if we're open. I've seen men and women who initially felt understood and encouraged when they took these inventories, but when opportunities came to them months later, they disqualified themselves because they said, "This doesn't fit who I am." We aren't static; we're wonderfully dynamic and connected to the infinitely creative and powerful Spirit, who is full of possibilities. The inventories are snapshots, not movies of our lives. The tools can accurately reflect who we are at a particular moment, but they don't necessarily account for where God might want to take us in the future.

If you're a nurturing leader, invite your futuring team to bring a fresh vision of the future so you can invest your compassion better and more widely. Your job is to value them, celebrate their insights, and involve them in the plan to take advantage of their work. If you're a futuring leader, release the specialized leaders on your team to bring you a wealth of specifics about what they see in the distance. Your job is to mesh their specifics into your big vision of the future and invite them to help you craft a grand plan to fulfill the needs you and your team have identified.

I believe the futuring team needs to gather at least once a year for a series of several meetings, and these meetings should conclude a month before the annual leadership retreat where they'll make their presentation.

Before the series begins, the members of the team research the latest trends, and they come together to give their giraffe views of what they see in the distance. They don't need to anticipate what might happen in ten years, or even five. Three years is the most foresight we can expect with any degree of accuracy. A three-year plan is legitimate; beyond that is pure speculation.

> If you're a nurturing leader, invite your futuring team to bring a fresh vision of the future so you can invest your compassion better and more widely.

In this series of meetings, the team can use the four-part planning process (described in chapter 4). In the first couple of meetings, they don't make any decisions. They talk; they dream; they imagine what might be. Only after they've defined the opportunities and challenges clearly can they begin to craft specific plans. At the end of the planning process, they make a presentation, perhaps to the organization's leaders at the annual retreat or another significant meeting.

Change happens much more quickly in some fields than others. For instance, in education, change happens slowly; but in IT, it happens at the speed of light. I still recommend annual futuring meetings for leaders in education, but communication and technology may have dramatic advances every day. I recommend futuring meetings at least twice a year, and maybe four times a year, for the technology sector. Whatever the time horizon for a field, each one needs to anticipate the problems. These problems, rightly anticipated, become wide doors of opportunity for the organization. Every successful pastor initially saw unmet needs and dove in to meet those needs. Every entrepreneur identified problems and created systems to meet the challenges. Problems aren't the problem; they're signals to pay attention and craft creative solutions.

> Problems aren't the problem; they're signals to pay attention and craft creative solutions.

Another way to look at the issue of anticipation is to ask, "What will happen if we do nothing, but we keep doing just what we're doing now?" This may not have been a piercing question during the Dark Ages, when change happened so slowly it was imperceptible, but leaders today must learn to ask it often. If we pack our suitcases for where we've been or where we are, we almost certainly won't be prepared for the cold winds and sunny skies of the future.

UNPACKING AND PACKING

Leaders who are too wedded to the past spend a lot of time warning people about the threats in the culture and the dangers of change in the organization. They are defensive and reactionary. Those who are focused on the present are comfortable with the status quo and are thrilled with incremental growth. But those who are committed to the future analyze what *will* be and dream about what their organizations *might* be. They don't start with a plan; they start with a ruthless analysis of the challenges in the future, which generates passion and sees anticipated problems as golden opportunities.

Part of the process of unpacking, then, is being honest about the possibility that the culture we've created—with great care over many years—is focused on the past or the present more than on the future. We can't just tell people we're implementing a radical new vision that will change everything. We must impart that vision with patience, persistence, energy, and emotion. They take their cues from us: if we aren't hemorrhaging for the vision to become a reality, they're not going to bleed.

When we read the newspaper, journals, and books, we may conclude our organizations must become as complex as our culture. But people are looking for clarity, not complexity. We need to have a crystal-clear vision with a singular focus. Yes, growing organizations are necessarily complex in their systems and structure, but those should always be servants to the driving vision, which must remain clear and compelling. No matter how large we grow, and no matter how intricate our communication systems may become, our message to the people in our communities must be clear enough to grip their hearts.

Our staffing—selection, placement, and development—should be done with an eye to the future. Too many leaders pick people to fill slots to meet immediate needs. This is shortsighted. Instead, we need to conduct a rigorous process to find people who will meet

> People are looking for clarity, not complexity.

the needs in the future. The right people won't be satisfied with today. They'll have a drive that will propel them to accomplish far more than incremental progress. As we select, we don't merely look at history and credentials. We give more weight to insight, vision, maturity, and passion. And in our training and development, we're always filling each person's suitcase with information, skills, and connections to prepare them for the higher challenges they'll face.

One of the most important steps a leader can take is to unpack and repack the organization's board. Sometimes this means unpacking some people and replacing them with others who have a longer vision—replacing moles and turtles with giraffes—but most of the time, the leader simply applies the staff-development strategies to the people on the board. In many cases, their focus and scope changes from financial oversight to becoming full, participating partners in the dynamic future of the organization. Ask board members to analyze emerging trends in the demographics of the community and the culture. Cultivate in them the skill to pack for the future.

An important part of communicating with the audience of the future is to take a hard look at our words. Are we speaking the language of the people we want to reach, or are we using "insider" words? Businesses typically do an excellent job of tailoring their language to their intended customers, but church leaders need to ask: Who is our audience? Do we craft our image, our environment, and our message to make irreligious people feel at least relatively comfortable when they walk through the

> Too many leaders pick people to fill slots to meet immediate needs.

doors of our churches? Many of us have lived in the Christian subculture so long that we don't know how to speak the language of the people who seldom walk through our doors.

When my wife and I pack for a trip overseas, we go through a deliberate process to be sure we have everything we need. (Her process is a lot longer than mine, but I don't need to explain that.) In the same way, unpacking and packing an organization's suitcase can't be rushed or we'll leave out some things that are vital for the trip to the future. In this case, speed is overrated. Insight, care, and patience will fill your suitcase with the right things so you'll be fully prepared.

If we're not prepared, we can be knocked off the road or stopped in our tracks. No matter how well we anticipate the future, we'll always encounter the unknown. Count on it, it's guaranteed. Fragile leaders won't make it, and lonely leaders won't make it very far. We need to build our spiritual, emotional, and relational muscles to be strong when we face the inevitable adversity.

Do you believe God has greater things in store for you in the future? Of course you do, or you wouldn't be a leader. Many of us, though, feel stuck and frustrated. The good news is that we don't have to stay stuck any longer. We can learn to anticipate the future and be ready for it.

In his tenure as the first chief engineer for the American effort to dig the Panama Canal, John Wallace felt paralyzed by congressional delays, miles of red tape to get any supplies, and the pressure to make progress despite his lack of resources. He complained of "system gone to seed" and the insistence to "make the dirt fly" without an adequate and comprehensive plan.[4] He couldn't take it, so he resigned and left Panama.

When John Stevens took over, he exemplified the two metaphors in this chapter. First, he realized his suitcase wasn't packed with the systems and structure required to complete the task. He had a giraffe's vision of the future fulfillment of the project, so he carefully packed his organizational suitcase with everything he would need to get there. He had to spend time to unpack and repack his systems and structures. He changed plans to construct locks instead of pursuing a sea-level plan, and then his engineers designed locks and gates for ships of the future. He was, at least for a while, a brilliant leader who packed for the future.

Are you a giraffe?

What's in your suitcase?

THINK ABOUT THIS

Reflect on these questions and discuss them with your team:

1. What are some advantages giraffes have over other animals? What are some reasons great leaders must be giraffes?

2. Are you a nurturer or a futurer? Explain your answer. Which type of leader would your staff or key volunteers say you are?

3. How would a futuring team help you? Who would be on it? How would it work?

4. Is your organization staffed for the past, the present, or the future? Explain your answer.

5. What's in your suitcase? What needs to be in your suitcase to take your organization where you believe it needs to go?

6. What process will you go through to unpack and repack?

Remember: The size and speed of an organization are controlled by its systems and structures.

CHAPTER 6

YOU DIDN'T EXPECT THIS, DID YOU?

At countless points in the story of the construction of the Panama Canal, optimism was shattered by harsh realities. The French were very confident the hero of Suez, Ferdinand de Lesseps, could build a similar canal across the isthmus in less time and at lower cost than at Suez. In fact, officials saw the project as more of an investment opportunity than a difficult engineering feat. At a congress in Paris in 1879, only 42 of the 136 delegates were engineers. The rest were politicians, speculators, and people who had blind faith in de Lesseps. The original cost

Mosquito Exterminator

estimate for the project was $214 million, but the overconfident de Lesseps and his engineers lowered the estimate several times to about half that amount. They believed it would take only six years to complete the canal, less time than it took to dig through the desert sand at Suez.

When construction began in 1881, the men encountered almost continual mudslides that buried men and machines, torrential rains, a raging river, rusting equipment, and stifling heat in the Central American jungle.

But these difficulties didn't compare to the plague of sickness and death from malaria and yellow fever. As we've seen, more than twenty-two thousand people died, including five thousand French engineers and members of their families.

After eight long and frustrating years, the French had spent more than their original estimate, but they had completed only 40 percent of the work. Bankruptcy was followed by scandal. The lofty expectations of the French people were shattered. No one had anticipated the size and scope of the difficulties they faced in Panama.

When Roosevelt renewed the vision for the canal, he encountered opposition from the Colombians, who, not surprisingly, wanted to keep control over their own land. To solve this pesky diplomatic problem, Roosevelt instigated a revolution. Panama became a sovereign nation and signed a treaty granting the United States rights to the Canal Zone. For the United States, things seemed to be falling together very easily.

As work began in the Canal Zone, the engineers faced daunting logistical problems, but the engineering problems weren't the only thing the engineers and workers faced in Panama. Disease stalked every person every day. The Americans were very aware of the deaths suffered during the French effort, and in the early years of American oversight, it appeared they would experience the same fate. The living conditions were deplorable. Thousands of workers lived in rotting shanties on stilts over swamps covered in green scum, with no sewage facilities except the water below. The stench was overpowering, and the water held the perfect breeding conditions for insects of all kinds.

Roosevelt soon realized sanitary conditions at the canal were of utmost importance. Men with fevers or in coffins couldn't perform extraordinary engineering feats. A doctor at Johns Hopkins recommended a physician who currently served in the army, Colonel William Crawford Gorgas. A few years earlier, an English doctor in India discovered that malaria wasn't caused by "vapors" as many believed. His research on the *Anopheles* mosquito showed the direct connection between the insect—specifically, the female of the insect—and people who contracted the disease. It was discovered that another species of mosquito, *Stegomyia fasciata*, carried yellow fever. With this information, Gorgas inaugurated an extensive fumigation program in Havana in 1901, virtually eliminating both malaria and yellow fever.

When Gorgas arrived at the Canal Zone in June 1904, he quickly realized the mosquitoes that carry yellow fever bred in stagnant water generally created by people where they worked or lived, but the insects that caused malaria were everywhere on the isthmus—man-made or natural environments—in enormous numbers. Gorgas explained to his staff that malaria was their primary target, but both diseases proved to be virulent. Gorgas planned to fumigate on a scale never imagined before. Every swamp, every stagnant pool, and every ditch had to be sprayed regularly to kill mosquitoes and their eggs and larvae.

The following year, he asked Congress for the astronomical sum of $1 million for the equipment and the manpower to cover almost five hundred square miles of jungle and swamp. Some lawmakers balked at the request, but Roosevelt's personal physician told him, "You are facing one of the greatest decisions of your career. If you fall back on the old methods you will fail, just as the French failed. If you back Gorgas you will get your canal."[1]

By 1906, more than 85 percent of workers had been hospitalized at some point. John Wallace's auditor died from yellow fever, and Wallace was so sure he would die that he had his casket built and ready for his demise. People became so frightened that three-fourths of the Americans in the Canal Zone fled during "the Great Scare." The fear wasn't calmed when it was reported that a man had died from bubonic plague. Gorgas then added trapping rats to his efforts to fumigate many square miles of shantytowns, jungles, and cities.

Still, Gorgas's efforts began to show promising results. By August 1906, the monthly number of yellow fever patients was cut in half, and in September only seven new cases appeared at the hospitals. On November 11, the last victim of yellow fever in the Canal Zone died. Malaria was more difficult to control, but by 1910, the death rates from this disease would drop to less than 1 percent.

Dr. Gorgas's methods of controlling insect-borne disease proved to be a monumental breakthrough for the world's population—perhaps more significant than completing the canal. The Panama Canal saved money in shipping, but the new method of fumigation saved thousands of lives. Roosevelt and Gorgas had faced the greatest threat to their work in the form of tiny but lethal insects, and they found a way to accomplish their mission.

NOT SO INSIGNIFICANT

When the Americans arrived at the Canal Zone, they saw huge scars in the earth at Culebra where the French had worked so hard to claw away a mountainside. They also looked at almost fifty miles of cleared jungle. The French progress had taken monumental effort, but the Americans also understood thousands of people had died from dreaded diseases. It had only recently been discovered that the cause of these diseases was insects that weigh only about 2.5 milligrams, or .000088 ounces. The mosquitoes look so small, but one bite could be a matter of life and death. When I was in Nigeria a few years ago, a wise person told me, "Whoever has mocked the size of a mosquito has never tried to sleep with even a single mosquito inside a mosquito net."

Leaders have mosquito problems too. We face seemingly insignificant "bites" of setbacks and opposition that can turn healthy environments into sick ones. In every organization, "mosquitoes" are more than annoying; they create fear and distrust, distract people from their tasks, and can wreck the whole endeavor. At the canal, the insects—the diseases they spread or the fear of sickness and death—affected every person from the lowest laborer to the chief engineer, as well as their families. In our businesses, churches, and nonprofits, they affect every person listed on the organizational chart and the people at home who try to help them with the stress. No one is immune.

World health organizations report that mosquitoes cause more disease and death around the globe than any other pest. These tiny demons not only spread malaria and yellow fever, but also Zika, West Nile virus, chikungunya, dengue fever, filariasis, and several forms of encephalitis. Each year almost seven hundred million people contract disease caused by mosquitoes, resulting in more than a million deaths.

What are the mosquitoes in our organizations? Simply understood, mosquitoes are bad attitudes, and carriers are those who are infected by these attitudes and spread them. We need to do a thorough analysis much like the one Dr. Gorgas conducted. We may have assumed our organizational problems come from vapors in the air, but actually, mosquitoes have bitten and infected people. They then become carriers, who have the potential to infect even more people.

The individual bites may not appear dangerous at all. In fact, they are almost imperceptible. If we look closely, though, we can see the damage. Each bite can infect our employees, staff, and volunteers with a con-

> What are the mosquitoes in our organizations?

tagious, negative attitude that surfaces in countless ways. Let me list some of the most common mosquitoes I've seen in organizations:

- Passive-aggressive behavior
- Unresolved conflict and resentment
- Gossip and secret alliances
- Poor communication that produces chronic misunderstanding
- Lack of accountability
- Failure to meet deadlines
- "Yes, but" resistance
- Refusing to be honest during a meeting but later criticizing decisions in private meetings
- Being a know-it-all
- Insisting, "It's your fault, not mine"
- Jealousy: "I want the status you have"
- Envy: "I want the things you have"
- Unhealthy competition
- And many others

The nature of infectious disease is that the smallest droplet that contains a contagious microorganism can affect a healthy person. In our organizations a pleasant, productive, optimistic person can join a team, but the bites of others infected with negativity and lethargy can cause that person to lose heart. He or she may try to fight off the effects for a while, but sooner or later that once-healthy team member stops turning work in on time, becomes irresponsible, and competes with others to see who can be the most sarcastic.

Mosquitoes have power to consume and control. Before every meeting, people on the team think about the carrier's potential reactions; during the meeting, they look closely to read that person's nonverbal communication; and after the meeting, they think about how to get the carrier on their side. For the leader, the carrier and the threat of infectious mosquitoes become the dominant filter to think about how to communicate the vision, plan the next steps, delegate responsibility, and hold people accountable. The vision and the communication are tailored to lessen the impact of the mosquito instead of achieving the blue-sky dreams of the organization.

MOSQUITOES IN SCRIPTURE

In the Bible we see many examples of individual and organizational devastation caused by mosquito bites: Eve listened to one lie from Satan. Jacob deceived his father one day and spent years on the run from his brother. His wife Leah suffered as she was compared to her beautiful sister Rachel. Moses sometimes felt overwhelmed by the complaints of the people as he led them through the desert to the promised land.[2]

> Mosquitoes have power to consume and control.

Perhaps the best example of the lethal impact of a single mosquito occurred when Joshua brought the children of Israel across the Jordan into the promised land. God performed a miracle of deliverance at Jericho.

Nothing, it seemed, could stop God's people from taking the land. God instructed Joshua to send three thousand men to take the hamlet of Ai, but when they attacked they were defeated in a shocking loss. The people of Ai "chased the Israelites from the city gate as far as the stone quarries and struck them down on the slopes. At this the hearts of the people melted in fear and became like water" (Josh. 7:5). Unable to figure out what happened, Joshua blamed God and wished they had stayed in the desert!

The problem, God explained, was that someone had disobeyed God and violated his covenant. A single mosquito was responsible for the tragic defeat. He told Joshua to gather all the people. The next morning they lined up tribe by tribe. God revealed the tribe, the clan, the family, and the man who had sinned. It was Achan. Exposed and guilty in front of Joshua and all the people, he admitted he had selfishly stolen some things during the attack. Joshua took care of the problem swiftly and clearly, and order was restored to the advance into the land God had promised them (vv. 6–26).

On another occasion, centuries later, the disease of superiority and exclusion threatened to derail God's plans for the fledgling church. Paul and Barnabas had seen the Spirit work in the lives of Gentiles on their first journey to tell people about Jesus, but when they brought the news back to Jerusalem, some Jewish leaders in the church firmly believed the Messiah was their own—and no one else's. They required Gentiles who believed in Christ, people they considered to be outsiders, to be circumcised and follow the Mosaic laws so they could become insiders.

Paul and Barnabas explained that God didn't view classes of believers as insiders and outsiders, first class and second class. God works miracles indiscriminately, and all who believe are equal in his kingdom. After a debate, James, the leader of the council, announced his decision that the Gentiles would be fully accepted as equals in the family of God. His pronouncement stopped the divisiveness that would have severely stunted the growth of the church. We can confidently say that the church would have been a lot different in the last two thousand years if the mosquitoes of superiority and exclusion hadn't been fumigated by the all-encompassing grace of God (Acts 15:1–35).

NETS AND FUMES

How long does it take a healthy person to be infected by a mosquito in an organization? In most cases, the gestation period is only about three

> The leader's challenge is to notice the mosquitoes—and the carriers—before they can infect others.

months. We may not see the full-blown symptoms for another month or two, but at that point we begin to see the devastating impact of the mosquito's microorganisms on the bitten person's attitude, cooperation, and effectiveness.

The leader's challenge is to notice the mosquitoes—and the carriers— before they can infect others. This foresight is rare, however. Most of us are slow to notice—and even slower to pass out netting—and slower still to fumigate.

Let me play the role of Dr. Gorgas and offer a solution to the problem with mosquitoes in our organizations:

1. *Identify the carriers.* Everyone has an occasional bad day, and everyone needs some grace to be forgiven for having a bad attitude once in a while; but in my experience with organizations all over the world, I've concluded that the vast majority of leaders are willfully blind to the buzzing going on all around them. Look for patterns, and look for impact. You may not be able to notice a bad attitude if the person is always pleasant in your meetings but critical in the hall afterward, but you can notice the person's persistently negative effect on others.

2. *Marginalize and quarantine.* For many reasons, you may not be ready to fire a division chief or a worship leader as soon as you notice the traits of infection, but you can reduce this person's influence in subtle ways. Take some responsibility away from the person, and give a higher profile to others on the team. Praise the positive impact of optimistic, responsible people.

3. *Offer the prospect of real change.* It doesn't work to beat around the bush too much, like making vague inferences or hints, when you're addressing this kind of problem with a person on your team. Have a heart-to-heart talk with the carrier to invite self-examination and change. Be honest about what you've seen and describe the specific problem. Describe what change looks like, and write out a standard of performance so you can both measure progress (or the lack of it).

4. *When necessary, fumigate.* When you've given a person a reasonable opportunity to change and he or she can't or won't—it doesn't matter which—it's time to say good-bye. Before this conversation, reflect on the very real consequences of dealing with the problem, as well as the consequences of not dealing with it. Consider the transitional issues that are deeper and wider than simply changing people and roles. This kind of decision inevitably produces a ripple effect among people who support that person and those who support you, and there will be unexpected and unintended consequences. Talk to those who need to be informed, perhaps your board, your HR director, and your executive staff. Be clear and brave.

5. *Oversee the healing process.* The female mosquito, which is the one that infects a person with a disease, may not live very long after the bite, but the one who is bitten needs time and care to recover. In the same way, you and your organization have been deeply affected by the mosquito. The impact probably won't be over soon. Be prepared, be diligent, and be persistent in applying the medicine of truth and grace to everyone touched by this person.

6. *Use preventive spraying.* Dr. Gorgas regularly and persistently sprayed mosquitoes, larvae, and eggs to be sure he got all generations of the insects. In our organizations, we need to consider spreading a preventative of truth and grace, and then reinstitute a vibrant, healthy culture to let people know we cannot tolerate carriers. We need to be careful to avoid being publicly critical of the person we let go, but we also need to be careful to avoid letting any other mosquitoes infect our teams.

When I was growing up in India, mosquitoes were a big problem. Most of the year we slept under nets covering our beds. For added protection, my parents gave us a pump sprayer full of repellant. Before we went to bed, we sprayed the net, our beds, under our beds, and anywhere else mosquitoes might hide before eating us for their dinner. The spray smelled awful, but avoiding the buzzing and the bites—and the threat of real sickness—made the smell easier to handle.

Like my parents, we should regularly spray honesty, love, optimism, truth, and a rigorous commitment to good communication on our teams. We watch for standing water of cynicism and gossip that is a breeding ground for insects, and we drain the swamp of unresolved conflict that is the perfect environment to hatch millions of eggs and spread disease. Sometimes we're quick enough to identify an infected carrier before mosquitoes make anyone else sick. An administrative assistant or a top executive—anyone can be a carrier. If we notice soon enough, this kind of sharp-eyed leadership solves a lot of problems before the eggs hatch.

None of us is above the possibility of being a carrier in our organizations. People of integrity are always willing to ask, "Is it me? Did I contribute to the problem in some way?"

DON'T BE SURPRISED

A friend of mine lives near Houston. He related that several years ago a tropical storm blew through, dumping more than twenty inches of rain on his community. The next day the skies cleared, the sun came out, and the creeks began to go back to their normal levels. About four days later, however, he walked out into his yard and had an uneasy feeling. He looked over into the bushes, and it appeared they had grown fur. He leaned over to take a closer inspection, and he realized that surrounding every branch of every bush, and in fact, all through the grass in his lawn, were millions and millions of mosquitoes! Even the slightest breeze or shake of the bushes unleashed swarms of the bloodsucking little monsters.

We need to realize that certain conditions in our organizations explode the population of mosquitoes. No matter how much we notice them and fumigate regularly, we'll always have a few—and in stormy times of organizational stress, they'll multiply and swarm. When we share a new vision for size and speed, our plans to update and restructure the systems and structure shake the bushes of our businesses, churches, and nonprofits. At the Panama Canal, the process of digging created even more pools of water for mosquitoes to breed. Our process of widening our canals also inevitably produces the natural elements of human nature: insecurity, fear, defensiveness, pride, and blame.

> People of integrity are always willing to ask, "Is it me? Did I contribute to the problem in some way?"

Don't be surprised when your boldest, most carefully considered plans result in a swarm of mosquitoes. The answer isn't to throw away the plans and go back to the status quo. We need to move forward, but with more insight. Our question must be: What in our culture is a breeding ground for mosquitoes?

Let me share a few observations I've made as I've consulted with leaders over the years:

- Most people get excited about a bold vision, but many are afraid they'll be lost or they'll fail in the steps of change. That's why they react negatively to the prospect of change.
- People are more afraid of *change that remains mysterious* than *change they understand*. Known misery is preferable to unknown glory, so it's almost impossible to over-communicate the process and the value of change.
- Every person reacts to change based on the assumptions created in his or her past experiences. Understand people's experiences and you can anticipate their responses.
- When people ask questions during times of change, don't assume

they're attacking you. They just need information and lots of reassurance.

- Our task as leaders is to paint a picture of a preferred future for our entire organization and to help each individual stakeholder understand it, anticipate the benefits, and own it.
- People thrive on a combination of hope and personal affirmation—not one or the other.
- If you see one mosquito, there are a hundred more you don't see.
- Trust is indispensable, so no matter what, tell your people the truth.
- Use rules to set a standard of excellence, but don't overuse them to control people. Those who need rigid rules to do their jobs are either new to the roles or carriers.
- It's important to clarify the chain of command so communication flows smoothly and directly. Questions and disagreements aren't problems in healthy environments, but they need to be directed toward the people who can make informed decisions.
- Too much agreement is a sign of stagnant communication that breeds mosquitoes. Some people are "conflict avoidant," which often comes out in their willingness to smile and nod even though they disagree. It occurs in some businesses but is rampant in churches and nonprofits. This kind of behavior looks "nice," "pleasant," and "thoroughly Christian" on the outside, but it doesn't promote rigorous dialogue and healthy debate that produce deep relationships and the best decisions.

DRAINING THE SWAMP

I've watched some remarkable leaders during times of change in their organizations. These men and women learned to be bilingual, speaking the language of bold vision and tender compassion to help people take steps toward that vision. In conversations with staff members, board members, and key volunteers, they haven't bullied their way to get others to comply. Instead, they built trust and understanding by using statements like these:

- "Help me understand what you're asking."
- "Can I push back on that a little bit? What you're saying is important to me."
- "I'm sorry. I didn't make that clear enough."
- "Can we get to the solution side of this problem?"
- "I'm sure you all noticed there's an elephant in the room we're not talking about. It's time for us to talk about it."
- "Now, let me give you the punch line to all I've been saying. This may be hard for some of you to hear, and I know you'll have questions. Let me explain first, and then you can ask anything you want to ask."
- "Are we okay with each other? It's fine to disagree, you know."

Teams can go through almost anything if they trust each other, but they can't enjoy even stunning success without it. Trust is the glue that holds relationships and organizations together, and it's the pipe that drains the swamp of suspicion and blame where mosquitoes breed. Trust is built as people prove to be honest when it would be convenient to shade the truth, dependable when it would be easy to let something go, kind instead of harsh or running away, and committed to excellence when we might be tempted to get by with "good enough." Some people value different relational traits of love, authenticity, and generosity more than the others, but all are important—on a team, in a family, or among friends.

Trust doesn't just happen, and we can't assume people start with a full cup to share. In fact, almost everybody comes to our teams with painful experiences of broken trust, strained relationships, and shattered dreams. Trust is always earned; it's not a right. Leaders pay a "trust tax" for every person who joins the team, as well as everyone who comes from a church where they were dissatisfied in any way. Most of the people we interact with each day have trust deficiencies. They don't feel valued, and we are

> Teams can go through almost anything if they trust each other.

one of the only sources—if not the only source—they have of stability and affirmation.

Be aware that the lowest-paid people in your organization control your brand and reputation more than the highest-paid people—because they interact with customers and visitors more than the top-level staff do. If they trust you, their positive perspective will spread out to the people they touch. If they don't trust you—if they come from a swamp of distrust and haven't yet been transformed by grace and truth—they'll be carriers unleashing mosquitoes that infect other people before you have any chance to connect with them.

YOUR OWN MOSQUITOES

If we're honest, we will admit that our thoughts have plenty of mosquitoes flying around. These pesky insects may be persistent worries, our own insecurities and fears of not measuring up, and comparison that leads to cycles of superiority (when we think we're doing better than others) and inferiority (when we feel like failures). Dedicated leaders are often plagued with the dark side of being driven: they live under an oppressive cloud of "shoulds."

Here's the truth: your happiness and effectiveness are inversely proportional to the "shoulds" in your life. The "shoulds" seem like reasonable benchmarks, but whenever we achieve our highest goals, we raise the bar even higher. In this way, we're never doing enough, being kind enough, praying enough, inspiring enough, or serving selflessly enough.

> Many wonderful leaders live in bondage to their "shoulds."

These thoughts and fears may buzz in our minds a hundred times a day, but we're so used to them we don't even notice their power to infect us. I believe many wonderful leaders live in bondage to their "shoulds." We would be far happier, less distracted, and more secure if we learn to apply the grace we teach to the deepest swamps in our own hearts.

The men who served as chief engineers at the canal realized the dangers posed by the mosquito-borne diseases. Dr. Gorgas's revolutionary methods saved thousands of lives. But these leaders also faced another daunting adversary. This one wasn't insidious; it was organized and institutional: the United States Congress. We'll look at this opposition in the next chapter.

THINK ABOUT THIS

Reflect on these questions and discuss them with your team:

1. What are some of the signs of mosquitoes in your organization?
2. Who are (or were) the carriers? What impact are they having (or did they have)? What took you so long to notice and address the issue?
3. Look at the steps outlined in this chapter to deal with mosquitoes. Which of these steps are you confident in taking? Which ones make you hesitant? Explain your answer.
4. What are some steps and language you can use to drain the swamp and build trust in your organization? How can they become a normal part of your culture? What difference will they make?
5. Do you have any mosquitoes flying around your mind and heart? (Of course you do!) What are they? How can you kill them and drain your own swamp that breeds them?

Remember: The size and speed of an organization are controlled by its systems and structures.

CHAPTER 7

HOW DO YOU HANDLE OPPOSITION?

When Americans arrived in Panama to begin the canal project again, they weren't at all surprised by the danger posed by mosquitoes. Doctors had only recently begun to understand the cause of malaria and yellow fever, and they had experimented with new techniques to eradicate the insects. The engineers expected disease and deaths—perhaps not on the scale suffered by the French and their workers, but the danger was real and inescapable. However, the engineers who were devoting their expertise, their energies, and time away from their families didn't expect opposition from a source they believed would be their biggest supporter: the United States Congress.

John Stevens
LIBRARY OF CONGRESS

When Wallace took over as chief of operations, he had every reason to expect the US government to provide for every need—speedily, eagerly, and generously. Instead Congress retained the right to debate the appropriation of every dollar and determine every major engineering decision. Even when Dr. Gorgas asked for money to fumigate the zone and save countless lives, it took the intervention of President Roosevelt to prod Congress to agree.

Wallace was desperate for help, so when a new Isthmian Canal Commission (ICC) was created, he recommended Theodore Perry Shonts, an attorney and railroad executive, to be the head of the commission. Roosevelt had wanted Elihu Root, his friend and a gifted former secretary of war, to take the role. Roosevelt asked Root to name his salary if he would accept, but Root refused because he believed the canal project was a black hole, a disaster no matter who was in charge. When Root backed out, Roosevelt tapped Shonts for the role.

Instead of providing assistance, Shonts became another layer of impediment between Wallace and Congress. The enormous stress of living in Panama, the struggle to get enough equipment and men to do the job, and the unrelenting expectations to make more progress more quickly exhausted Wallace. Finally, when "the Great Scare" caused him to worry about his safety and the safety of his family, Wallace had had enough. He was willing to stay on the job, he explained, but only if he was named chairman of the ICC to replace Shonts, was given complete control over the decisions regarding the canal, and received a large increase in salary.

Wallace went to Washington to meet with William Howard Taft, the secretary of war and Roosevelt's best friend, to complain and make his demands. The conversation didn't go well for Wallace. Taft reminded him of his commitments and expressed his deep disappointment in his attitude. Though Wallace had made demands without the threat to resign, Taft talked to Roosevelt about the situation, and the two men agreed to accept Wallace's implied resignation.

John Stevens was immediately selected to replace Wallace, and as we've seen, he made remarkable progress. His comprehensive vision to complete the project was coupled with skilled planning and relentless execution. In November 1906, Roosevelt visited the zone to see the work in progress. His visit was a stunning success, and he left with the utmost confidence in Stevens. The new chief engineer had designed and implemented more efficient systems for the steam shovels and trains, and work at Culebra Cut was moving ahead faster than ever.

However, things quickly changed. On a visit to Washington the next month, Stevens turned from the confident Dr. Jekyll into a fierce and sullen Mr. Hyde. He wanted to have Dr. Gorgas fired, and even the brilliantly persuasive Roosevelt found him impossible to please. A few weeks later, when Stevens was back at the canal, he wrote a long and impassioned letter to the president. He was bitter and blunt. He described "enemies in the rear" and the travails of being "continually subject to attack by a lot of people . . . that I would not wipe my boots on in the United States."[1] He identified at least some of "these people" as members of Congress. He complained that the personal sacrifice simply wasn't worth the price he was paying as the chief engineer.[2] Like Wallace, this letter didn't include the explicit threat to resign if his demands weren't met—in fact, there were no demands, only complaints. The president and Taft discussed this unusual letter, and as they did with Wallace, they decided to accept the implied resignation.

Two gifted, dedicated, experienced chief engineers broke under the oppressive constraints and delays caused by government officials they had expected to give them all the help they needed. Wallace and Stevens thought members of Congress would be their allies, but they became their enemies.

Roosevelt needed the very best people to hold his ladder so he could reach his goal of completing the canal. Wallace looked like the perfect choice, but he couldn't stand the strain. Stevens made far more progress, but he, too, had limitations. Would Roosevelt ever find someone competent and dedicated enough to hold his ladder?

THE INEVITABILITY OF OPPOSITION

Sooner or later, every grand, bold vision encounters significant opposition. We may assume that opposition is always destructive, but it can be a powerful force that crystallizes our imagination, focuses our plans, and drives us to succeed. An airplane uses the opposition of the air to enable it to fly. Millions of us use weights in our exercise program because the resistance makes us stronger. Teachers give their students problems and exercises to force them to think more clearly, understand principles, and discover answers. Tests aren't designed to make people fail but to propel them to learn and grow. In the same way, exceptional leaders use opposition as tests to sharpen them and equip them to reach even higher.

I find it helpful to distinguish between resistance and ridicule. Resistance is disagreement, and it often comes in the form of opposition to an idea or a plan, but ridicule is a personal attack. Resistance may be intellectual or procedural, but ridicule has a strong emotional component. A person who resists may ask, "I don't understand why you want to do that. It doesn't make sense to me. Would you explain why you want to do it?" But ridicule mocks, "What fool would want to do it that way?" Our response to people depends on our interpretation of their opposition: Are they asking for more information, or are they trying to harm us?

> Every grand, bold vision encounters significant opposition.

When people push back on my ideas, it causes me to think more clearly and articulate my ideas with more precision. In the process of give and take, I discover who is open to the new information and becomes a partner in the effort—and who doesn't care how much sense it makes and becomes an adversary. All of us can handle resistance far better than we cope with ridicule.

Every heroic character in the Bible experienced either resistance or ridicule, or both. Family members lied to them and deceived them, and close friends betrayed them. They suffered attacks by enemies, and they had to deal with pride and fear in those who claimed to be their supporters. Jesus, the Creator, King, and Savior, who loved people to the utmost, was abandoned by his friends, betrayed by one of them, denied by another, falsely accused by those who knew the Scriptures better than the rest of the people did, and flogged, beaten, and mocked by soldiers, the crowd, and the religious leaders. And then, at the supreme moment of Jesus' agony, the Father turned his back on him as he hung on the cross so he could bear the punishment for the sins of the world. For Jesus, the worst opposition a man has ever endured led to a cleansing flood of forgiveness, a glorious resurrection, and hope for all humankind.

Suffering may make us hard and bitter, but it can make us humble, tender, and wise. Paul learned to be content in the full range of situations. His trust in the sovereignty and wisdom of God gave him perspective on the opposition he faced. As a British pastor wryly commented, "Wherever St. Paul went, he started riots. Wherever I go, they serve tea."[3] In his second letter to the Corinthian believers, Paul gave them a brief catalog of heartaches that we can assume could have been much longer. He wrote:

> I have . . . been in prison more frequently, been flogged more severely, and been exposed to death again and again. Five times I received from the Jews the forty lashes minus one. Three times I was beaten with rods, once I was pelted with stones, three times I was shipwrecked, I spent a night and a day in the open sea, I have been constantly on the move. I have been in danger from rivers, in danger from bandits, in danger from my fellow Jews, in danger from Gentiles; in danger in the city, in danger in the country, in danger at sea; and in danger from false believers. I have labored and toiled and have often gone without sleep; I have known hunger and thirst and have often gone without food; I have been cold and naked. Besides everything else, I face daily the pressure of my concern for all the churches. (2 Cor. 11:23–28)

Suffering may make us hard and bitter, but it can make us humble, tender, and wise.

But Paul realized God had a purpose in his pain. In the same letter, he explained that the suffering he experienced at the hands of his opponents had given him far greater compassion for others who are hurting. He explained:

Praise be to the God and Father of our Lord Jesus Christ, the Father of compassion and the God of all comfort, who comforts us in all our troubles, so that we can comfort those in any trouble with the comfort we ourselves receive from God. For just as we share abundantly in the sufferings of Christ, so also our comfort abounds through Christ. If we are distressed, it is for your comfort and salvation; if we are comforted, it is for your comfort, which produces in you patient endurance of the same sufferings we suffer. And our hope for you is firm, because we know that just as you share in our sufferings, so also you share in our comfort. (2 Cor. 1:3–7)

Paul's distress came from his experience of both resistance and ridicule, and beyond what most of us will ever endure, he suffered physical torture and privation. As we move forward toward size and speed, we'll undoubtedly encounter opposition in various forms. Will it make us humbler, wiser, and gentler, or will it make us defiant, resentful, and hardened? We have a choice.

SOURCES OF OPPOSITION

Leaders face opposition from three distinct sources: *procedures*—how things are done; *prerequisites*—why things are done; and *personnel*—who gets things done. If we respond well, our experience of resistance can have benefits in all three areas. We will find better and more creative ideas to accomplish our objectives, better decisions are made because we've been forced to consider our reasons for all we do, and more people buy into the systems and processes because they have been part of the process of evaluation and planning. When our people feel heard and understood, they become committed to contribute to the success of the venture.

But ridicule often has the opposite impact. When we feel attacked and accused, we may become defiant, shutting down any chance for open, creative conversations. Emotions—ours and others'—overwhelm and clog the thinking process, so we react in fear or anger instead of pursuing sound judgments. The intense feelings make us either demanding or passive—or perhaps they even cause us to cycle through both. Resistance may eventually bring people closer, but ridicule often alienates and isolates. And of course, some of those who resist also ridicule, so we experience a double blow.

> Leaders face opposition from three distinct sources: *procedures*—how things are done; *prerequisites*—why things are done; and *personnel*—who gets things done.

Ridicule dishonors and demeans us. It has the potential to completely consume us with sleepless nights and worried or furious days. Some of us can't eat and we lose weight; others of us can't stop eating. We snap at people we love, and we avoid people who want anything from us. Some of us can't take it, so we give up and give in, no matter how unreasonable the demands may be.

Others drown themselves in distractions, like gambling, sports, pornography, or other amusements; numb themselves with alcohol or prescription drugs; or hide for hours on social media, to the point of not even showing up for work. But some refuse to back down; they fight back with ferocity, alienating even those who would be allies if the leader spoke the truth with less venom. Like Wallace and Stevens, we may come to a breaking point and simply give up.

We aren't alone in being ridiculed. At one point, people from Jesus' hometown discarded him as just "the carpenter's son" (Matt. 13:55) and powerful leaders insisted he was demon-possessed (Matt. 12:23–24). But Jesus knew perfectly who he was. He was secure in the Father's love, and he knew why he came to earth. He responded with grit, strength, clarity, and wisdom to every act of resistance and ridicule. His responses to his opponents, especially in John's gospel, are a model of how to engage adversaries with a blend of truth and grace.

How can we learn from Jesus' example? The answer isn't to just try harder, a solution that doesn't have lasting effects. We need to look deeper—at the source of Jesus' security and strength. He was thoroughly convinced that the Father adored him and had called him to a mission. No matter what he faced, nothing shook this bedrock truth. His self-concept wasn't based on the opinions of others. He knew what was in the human heart, so he wasn't surprised when some loved him, many feared him, and a few plotted to murder him.

A deep grasp of the love of God and confidence that his purposes never fail give us the foundation of a well-managed ego. With these, we can be confident without being cocky, patient without being passive, determined without being dogmatic, and assertive without being aggressive.

> We need to look deeper—at the source of Jesus' security and strength.

Many of us have been so busy talking about the love of God and driven to share it with more people that we've forgotten what it feels like to know we're cherished by the King of creation.

Resistance and ridicule force us to reevaluate the foundation on which we stand. Have we been trusting in our stellar performance and success? Is our supreme value the applause of others? Those are crumbling foundations. In the middle of opposition, we have an opportunity to dig down deeper and find more grace and security than ever before—not because the search is a good thing to do, but because we know we can't make it without a genuine experience of God's unfailing love.

RESPONDING TO RIDICULE

Years ago I rose from serving as the janitor at a Christian college to become the president. When I took the top position, we had eighty-seven students; when I left, we had more than eight hundred. During my tenure, we needed to find a way to achieve national accreditation. The executive director of one of the accrediting agencies was coming to Atlanta, so I asked him to come to our college to meet with me. By that time we had about two hundred students.

I invited everyone on my executive team to the meeting with him in my office. After listening to our proposal, he sat back in his chair and sneered,

"If somebody wrote you a check for $10 million today so you could buy everything you need, and if you had all the research and paperwork we require in my hands today, the process would take *at least six years* before our agency would grant accreditation!" He almost laughed at the thought. Clearly he believed it was ridiculous for us to even consider being accredited by his sterling organization. In fact, he left the distinct impression that any association with us would tarnish their reputation. This was foot-dragging resistance combined with scornful ridicule.

In a derisive tone, he then explained the three stages required: applicant, candidate, and accreditation. Typically, colleges need two years to complete their applicant status, then four to six years in candidate status to prove themselves worthy before being granted accreditation: the full stamp of approval. We hadn't spent the two years preparing our application, so we were six to eight years away, according to his projections.

Soon after this meeting, I learned that the US Department of Education had approved another accrediting agency. Suddenly the other organization had competition. The newly approved agency wanted to support colleges like ours, and we very much wanted their seal of authenticity to increase our credibility in the community and our ability to raise money. We were put on a fast track and accredited in only three years.

Shortly after we announced our new accreditation, I received a call from the executive director of the first agency, the man who had visited with us. We had been the fastest-growing Christian college in America for the previous three years, and it appears he realized his organization had been left behind. He came to our office and sat in the same chair in the same room with the same people on our executive team. He had been dismissive of us earlier, but his tone and expressions were very different now. He had asked for the meeting, so he began, "I see your college is doing very well. Congratulations!" We nodded our acceptance of his compliment, and he continued, "We'd like to work with you. We'd like to offer your college our accreditation."

I answered, "That would be wonderful. We'd be happy to have it in addition to the other one."

The executive director frowned and shook his head. It was clear he meant *instead of* the other agency. He said lowly and slowly, "But no other college in the country is accredited by both."

I smiled, "Then we will be the first."

It wasn't the answer he expected to hear. I didn't miss a beat. "A few years ago, you explained your process. Would you tell us again?"

He outlined the three stages of the process, and his timing for each one hadn't changed.

I told him, "We'd like to make application today. We'll fill out the forms and write you a check. I understand you have a meeting in three months to consider colleges that have applied. I'd like you to give us full accreditation at that meeting."

He looked stunned, but there must have been something in my demeanor that told him I wasn't joking. He shook his head and said to no one in particular, "We've never done anything like that before."

"That's okay," I responded. "That's what we'd like you to do."

And that's exactly what happened. I learned something very important from this series of interactions: the people who ridicule us are watching us closely to see if we'll get angry and defiant (the *fight* response) or cower in fear (the *flight* response). They seldom expect us to respond with strength, wisdom, grace, and creativity. Even in the first conversation, when he was so condemning, I didn't bark back at him. I didn't say what I really wanted to say! Instead, I thanked him for coming and giving us information, and I promised to stay in touch. I didn't close the door to future opportunities, no matter how we were being treated.

A year or two after we received our second accreditation and our college continued to grow, I drove back to campus one night for a meeting, but I couldn't find a parking place. There were so many students taking night classes after work that the campus was packed. I hadn't been on campus at night in some time, so I was quite surprised. I wondered if many students would rather come to classes before going to work instead of after.

In the coming days, I determined classes would need to start about six o'clock in the morning. I'd never heard of anyone trying this before. I went into the dean's office and told him my plan. He listened carefully and then roared with laughter. He thought I'd lost my mind! He smiled and asked, "Sam, what student is going to get up so early and come to class before a full day of work?" Then he stopped himself and asked, "Wait a minute. What professor is going to get up and drink enough coffee to be alert to teach a class at that hour?"

I told him, "If we're going to try this experiment, I want our very best professors to teach these classes, and we'll pay them more to honor their commitment. We're not cutting any corners."

When we offered the early classes the next semester, they were the first ones filled by eager students. Now a wife could come to class, her husband could drop their child off at day care, and they had their evenings together instead of one shuttling off to campus. The benefits were enormous for everyone involved.

The pushback from my dean wasn't ridicule. Most of us would be happy for a friend to laugh at our ideas. Instead, we don't get laughter; we get mocking, secret alliances, false accusations of misconduct, and the kind of opposition that threatens to drag us into the mud of despair.

IT COMES WITH THE TERRITORY

Every leader has a target on his or her back. It comes with the job. The bigger the vision, the more people sneer, mock, condemn, and accuse, and the more at least a few of them try to get in the way to block progress. Banks think we're fools for trying to borrow so much money to build a bigger facility to reach more people, community leaders mock our efforts to make a difference in parts of town others avoid, smart people make fun of us because we try to be clear and simple, and simple people dismiss us because we aren't afraid to explain the magnificent truths of God.

The closer our relationship to these people, the more resistance perplexes us and ridicule hurts us. It can come from our staff—and even from our best friends, our spouses, and our children. No, the problem certainly isn't all people, and not even most of them, but it only takes one tiny grain of sand in an eye to cause great discomfort—and sometimes we face sandstorms!

If we're not careful, all this opposition can erode both our faith in God and our self-confidence. We wake up one morning in a toxic cloud of doubt and assume, "They're probably right. This vision *is* foolish!" We second-guess what we heard from God, and we second-guess every decision we made from that time forward. Soon we begin whittling away the edges of the vision, downsizing so it doesn't threaten anyone's comfort level—and so no one asks more hard questions. Our strategy becomes appeasement: making others happy with us at all cost. The policy of appeasement weakened Britain and France when they gave in to Hitler before World War II, and it weakens us in our pursuit of God's grand vision for us.

> It only takes one tiny grain of sand in an eye to cause great discomfort— and sometimes we face sandstorms!

We've examined signs of strain that often occur when we face unrelenting resistance and ridicule. Let me outline a few more. When we feel opposed or attacked, we may

- insist that others acknowledge we're right, and insist they acknowledge they're wrong! Being right, however, is a poor substitute for being secure, kind, and thoughtful.
- feel compelled to control everything. To feel safe from turmoil caused by others' mistakes (or their creativity), we demand that every decision pass through us.
- nitpick others' decisions, and we excuse our decisions that proved to be misguided.
- label people as good or bad so we can fully accept them or fully discard them. That's easier, it seems, than seeing every person as a complex, multidimensional human being.
- engage in vicious, negative self-talk. We're angry at people, at God, and—maybe most of all—at ourselves.

- relive every important conversation and situation to conduct a thorough postmortem to assign blame. Every little comment or facial expression becomes monumental.
- seldom laugh because everything has the potential to be catastrophic.
- laugh at things that aren't funny.
- have our thoughts and our time consumed with handling the people who resist and ridicule.
- shade the truth—or tell outright lies—to avoid being opposed even more.
- assume we know how each person will respond before every meeting and conversation. Our fearful anticipation puts them and us in rigid boxes.
- begin to see every person as a potential enemy, even those who have been supportive.
- forget all about the vision for greater size and speed, and avoid plans for systems and structures because these are the dreams that have led to the nightmare.

When we're under the strain of resistance and ridicule, we often choose exactly the wrong solution: we double down on all these behaviors because they feel so logical and right. We need a better—and a very different— answer. We need to take time to step back, gain some perspective, realize we're digging the hole even bigger by these actions, and go deeper into our source of security and significance. Instead of putting our heads down and running over people who disagree with us, we can walk away for a while, talk to a friend or mentor to get a fresh perspective, and then wade back in with a powerful blend of humility (we don't know it all), love (those people may be acting out of their own insecurities too), and strength (I answer to God, and he will see me through).

In the process of restructuring our souls, we need a few good friends. Friends are those people who see the best in you and bring out the best in you. You can count on them to be supportive when the chips are down.

> When we're under the strain of resistance and ridicule, we often choose exactly the wrong solution.

True friends are on your side, but they're willing to say the hard things you don't want to hear. We don't need people who need us to need them, who will rush in to fix us and make us all better. We need people who are perceptive, are honest, and tell us the truth, no matter how painful it is to hear it. We may want to run away, but a true friend will help us find a way to keep standing. Our friends point out our defense mechanisms and self-destructive patterns of thinking and acting. They may not offer comfort—at least at first—but we need people like this to tell us the truth so we can clarify our choices.

Friends show us that opposition, and even genuine failure, isn't the end of the world. They remind us we've enrolled in a graduate program to learn life's most important lessons. All leaders walk this path of resistance and ridicule, and the great ones come out on the other side stronger and wiser.

How can we know if we've learned these lessons? At least one sure benchmark is our willingness to listen to people who used to annoy us. With a new depth of humility, we respect those at the lowest level of our organizations, and we value—but not necessarily agree with—the opinions of those who oppose us. We move toward those people so we can engage them, and we try to understand their point of view more than insisting they understand ours. For this to happen, we need to shut up, give eye contact, and ask plenty of good questions. Listening to others builds trust, just as insisting on our own way erodes trust. We may not win them to our

> Friends show us that opposition, and even genuine failure, isn't the end of the world.

side of the argument, but at least we have a better chance of both sides walking away from the conversation with less anger, a little more understanding, and perhaps an open door for the next talk.

Wallace and Stevens were exemplary engineers with backgrounds that equipped them for their roles to lead the work at the canal, but they couldn't handle the resistance and ridicule from Congress and officials from the Isthmian Canal Commission. In the next chapter, we'll see that Roosevelt finally found the right man for the job.

THINK ABOUT THIS

Reflect on these questions and discuss them with your team:

1. What are some examples of resistance you've faced as a leader? What are some examples of ridicule you've encountered? How did you handle them?

2. Do you believe opposition in both forms is inevitable for a leader? Explain your answer.

3. Look at the list of signs we're under strain from opposition. Which of these have you experienced? Which ones would your spouse or your closest friend say you've experienced? Describe the impact on your thinking, your health, your relationships, and your leadership.

4. Who is a friend you can count on? Who is someone who tells you the truth? If you don't have this person in your life, where will you find him or her?

5. Describe how a deeper experience of the love and purpose of God is essential if leaders are to avoid self-defeating behaviors and learn the lessons God wants them to learn.

Remember: The size and speed of an organization are controlled by its systems and structures.

CHAPTER 8

HOW CAN YOU MAKE YOUR SYSTEMS HUM?

A fter John Stevens complained so much that Secretary Taft decided to take the complaints as a resignation, Roosevelt needed to find someone who could complete the canal. The president was bitterly disappointed in Stevens, so disappointed that when Roosevelt wrote his autobiography and described the years of work on the canal, he didn't even mention him.

George Washington Goethals
LIBRARY OF CONGRESS

Roosevelt wanted a chief engineer with the same brilliance and dogged determination he had. He needed someone who wouldn't wilt under pressure, who had engineering expertise, leadership skills, and a steadfast commitment to overcome any obstacles. Secretary Taft knew just the man to recommend. Colonel George Washington Goethals had spent his career in the US Army Corps of Engineers. He began as a student at West Point and graduated second in his class. He was the same age as Roosevelt, who graduated Phi Beta Kappa from Harvard the same year. Goethals served under the celebrated general William Tecumseh Sherman in 1884 in Vancouver, Washington. Sherman believed he was the finest young officer in his command.

A year later, Goethals became an instructor in civil and military engineering at his alma mater. After four years, he went back into the field and designed a river lock with the highest lift ever constructed. By 1903, he was picked to be on the army's general staff. His specialty was coastal defenses. His demeanor was dignified, and he lived by the highest standards of ethical conduct and professionalism.

While Colonel Goethals was serving on the general staff, Secretary Taft noticed him. After Taft's painful and infuriating meeting with Stevens, he recommended Goethals to Roosevelt as Stevens's replacement. Roosevelt invited Goethals to the White House, and the president didn't waste any time. He proposed the reorganization of the canal commission, with Goethals to assume the dual positions of chairman of the commission and chief engineer—a combination of roles that Stevens had recommended earlier. The previously awkward relationship between the chief engineer and the commission was resolved instantly. In effect, Roosevelt was giving Goethals ultimate authority as "Czar of the Zone," reporting only to Taft and himself.

Some historians have surmised that Colonel Goethals was selected because Taft and Roosevelt wanted the army to control the effort at the canal, but it's more likely they were searching for a man of unquestioned dedication to the task—and that man happened to be a respected officer in the army. Goethals was absolutely dedicated to fulfill his duty, no matter the challenges he might face.

Goethals cared nothing for fame or fortune. He immediately went to work at the canal, but not before giving credit to Stevens for the advances he had produced in his tenure as chief engineer. He proved to be demanding but fair. His dignity and commitment filtered down to every aspect of the work and to every engineer and worker. He realized the thousands of workers needed information, and they needed to be heard.

Goethals started a weekly newspaper to share news from America and give updates on progress at the canal. He also created a court of appeals, with himself as the chief magistrate. He presided in his office every Sunday morning to listen to grievances, large and small, from anyone who wanted to tell him about a problem. Like Moses, he made himself available to listen to anyone among the forty thousand people on the payroll, regardless of role, nationality, ethnicity, or the pettiness of the complaint. But Goethals never let himself get bogged down by the requests. Every week, from the time he arrived in 1907 until the canal was completed in 1914, people could find him and talk with him on Sunday mornings in his office.

Roosevelt needed the right people in the right roles. Taft was brilliant, gifted, and a trusted friend. In Goethals, he and Taft finally had the right man to fulfill the dream of a path between the oceans. Who was chiefly responsible for building the canal? Three chief engineers and three presidents served between the revolution in Panama and the day when the first ship traversed the canal in 1914, but Goethals singled out one man. He wrote, "The real builder of the Panama Canal was Theodore Roosevelt." Roosevelt's impact on the completion of the canal couldn't have been more evident "if he had personally lifted every shovelful of earth in its construction."[1]

YOUR LADDER

In many ways, Theodore Roosevelt was a one-off human being, one of a kind, unique in the annals of history. Single-handedly, he dragged the United States into the twentieth century with remarkable vision, optimism, energy, wit, and tenacity. But all of us are like him in one important way: we need to find the right people to help us fulfill our dreams. No matter how beautifully we construct our systems to achieve more size and speed, we'll feel as though we're running in mud if we don't have the right people in our structures.

If leaders have unqualified people holding their ladders, they won't be able to climb very high. The ones who help us climb six feet up a stepladder may not be the ones who can hold it securely so we can climb twenty feet up an extension ladder. And the ones who help us climb twenty feet may not be the ones who have the strength, skill, and commitment to help us scale a forty-five-foot ladder. Even strong and talented people aren't helpful

> No matter how beautifully we construct our systems to achieve more size and speed, we'll feel as though we're running in mud if we don't have the right people in our structures.

if they get distracted, walk away, or worse, kick out the bottom of the ladder so it falls. Like Roosevelt, we may enlist people we hope will be right for our teams, but we may be disappointed. Our success with selection will be, at least to some degree, trial and error, but finding the right ones is essential. Nothing else will do.

How do you know if someone isn't the right person? Here's a clue: if someone on your team resigns or threatens to resign, accept it! When de Lesseps was done, Wallace took over but didn't make much progress. When he complained too long and too loud, Taft took his gripes as an implied resignation. Stevens implemented important improvements, but he, too, wilted under the strain. Taft interpreted Stevens's complaints as the desire to quit, and the secretary immediately accepted the implied offer. The long history of the canal to this point was a litany of brilliant leaders who failed miserably. Now things would be different. Goethals was unquestionably the right man for the job. In each instance, the resignations led to progress. Each time, systems and structures improved so the organization could reach higher toward the goals of size and speed. Each resignation created three things: a crisis point, an important decision for Roosevelt, and new opportunities for growth.

As organizations move forward, the people chosen as ladder holders may need different skills, more training, a more expansive background, wider perspectives, stronger discipline, better talents to process and communicate information, and greater commitment to the leader and the vision of the organization. This doesn't mean the people who served faithfully as the organization grew aren't valuable. They were God's gift to the leader and the company, church, or nonprofit. But they may not be equipped to hold the ladder as the leader takes the organization higher.

We don't discard those faithful, committed men and women. Instead, we make sure we find a place for them that fits their talents and capacity. At some point all of us reach the limit of our capacity, so limits aren't a character flaw in any way. Some people may not be on our team any longer, but they can serve incredibly well at the level we just left, where

> If someone on your team resigns or threatens to resign, accept it!

other leaders in our organizations are climbing higher—just not as high as our ladder. It is, I believe, a dictum of leadership to understand a simple but crucial principle about reaching your desired future: those who got you here may not be the ones to take you there.

The best leaders know how to bring out the best in their people, but they also understand how to enlist and use people from different backgrounds and disciplines. Roosevelt's first two ladder holders were civilians. Wallace and Stevens were highly regarded, but both faded under the intense strain. When Roosevelt chose Goethals, he found a man who refused to fade. He brought his military experiences to shape the existing systems and structures, and under his leadership the canal achieved the desired size and speed. Building the canal was still a civilian project, but Goethals's military training and tenacity made all the difference. We could identify quite a few differences between Goethals and his predecessors, but let me point out a few of the most important differences between military and civilian cultures:

MILITARY CULTURE	CIVILIAN CULTURE
Moves quickly	Moves slowly
Has a clear chain of command	Often has a complicated chain of command
Values quick decisions	Values slow and methodical analysis
Has little patience with delays	Expects delays
Little talk, much action	Much talk before action
Training before the task	Training during the task
Usually motivated by duty and honor	Often motivated by self-interest
Quick to replace incompetence	Slow to replace incompetence

Churches, businesses, and nonprofit organizations aren't the armed forces, but it may serve us well to at least look at the strengths of different cultures to see what we might learn from them. One of the principles we might learn from the military culture is that turning a blind eye to incompetence or a bad attitude inevitably leads to a disaster down the road.

I'm not insinuating that leaders need to clean house and fire every person on their teams every few years, but I'm recommending that leaders evaluate the capacity of each person on the team from time to time. As the ladder gets higher, the leader can clearly outline the job descriptions of the ladder holders for the next extension—and give each person on the team a choice. Some will choose to acquire greater skills and expand their capacity, but some won't or can't, so they need to be gently reassigned to a role that fits them. At a leadership roundtable, someone quoted one of the later *Dune* novels: "The capacity to learn is a gift. The ability to learn is a skill. The willingness to learn is a choice."[2]

When I talk to pastors, heads of nonprofits, and business leaders, I make the point with less artistic flair. I tell them every staff member needs to know: "If you don't grow, you've gotta go." It's a bit blunt, but it gets the message across.

It's never a mystery who needs to be let go and replaced in any organization. When I meet with leadership teams about the need for every person on the team to be growing so they can hold a higher ladder, I often ask this question: "If you could walk into the office tomorrow and fire one person—and there would be no consequences at all for you or the organization—do you know who you would fire?" I have yet to find any leader who didn't instantly say, "Of course!"

Every organization has somebody (or more than one somebody) who is obviously a drag on the culture, relationships, and effectiveness of the team—and has been a drag for much longer than anyone wants to admit. You don't have to be an HR specialist to know who this person is. If leaders don't act to first confront this person and offer a chance for improvement—and if there is no change, release the person—every

other person on the team has the right to
wonder, "Does the leader see what we see?
If he does, why doesn't he do something
about it?"

> It's never a mystery
> who needs to be let
> go and replaced in
> any organization.

It doesn't take long for trust to erode
when leaders are too timid to take necessary action. When leaders don't make
tough decisions about people who are a drag on their teams, they lose
leadership equity with the rest of the team. Every decision raises or low-
ers the leader's equity, and the refusal to address the elephant in the room
knocks a big hole in the bucket. At that point, equity doesn't seep out; it
flows out.

A PROCESS BEFORE A DECISION

Roosevelt and Taft gave Wallace and Stevens every possible resource
and opportunity, but when these engineers complained more than they
looked for new solutions to problems, Roosevelt and Taft made the hard
choices to replace them. Stevens was more competent than Wallace, but
he couldn't hold Roosevelt's ladder well enough. Both times, Roosevelt
and Taft carefully considered the situation,
but they didn't delay in making the change.
The vision for completing the canal made
them uncompromising in requiring excellence of their chief engineer.

> When leaders
> don't make tough
> decisions about
> people who are a
> drag on their teams,
> they lose leadership
> equity with the
> rest of the team.

We aren't uncaring when we require
growth from our people as our ladder
extends higher and higher. We're just being
reasonable that a bigger vision requires
greater skill and capacity from the members of our team. Someone who flies a
single-engine Cessna and one who flies

a 777 are both pilots, but they have very different skills and capacities. If a company buys the latest accounting software, they must train their people, or find new people, to get the most out of it.

In churches, this principle applies to worship leaders, small group coordinators, administration, sound systems, student ministries, men's and women's ministries, and every other aspect of church life and growth. In business, it applies to production, marketing, distribution, and all the elements under those headings. In every conceivable field, it's foolish to design magnificent systems and fail to anticipate the needed growth in the people—the organizational structure—to make the systems work. When we don't anticipate the growth needed for our people to use expanded systems, we set them up for failure and create headaches for ourselves. That's not a recipe for success!

As you read this chapter, I'm sure you're thinking of wonderful people who have been with you for years. They have been faithful and loyal, and they have put their blood, sweat, and tears into their work. They have proven to be competent workers, and they've become trusted friends. It's inconceivable to walk in and simply let them go—and I want to assure you, that's not what I'm recommending.

You know you need ladder holders at a higher level of competence, talent, and execution if you're going to climb higher. The solution is to institute a good process before you need to make any hard decisions. Let me offer some suggestions for this process:

Ask yourself, "As this person's leader, how can I help him grow in knowledge, skills, and passion?"

One of your primary roles is to equip and empower those you lead. How well are you performing this role? Equipping people involves training in skills, but it's more than that. We equip people to see their unique contribution to the greater vision so they're highly motivated every day. We also equip them to communicate well with everyone on the team and in their spheres of influence. We equip them to excel up and down the chain of command and with all their peers. We empower them with clear direction and authority to get their jobs done—without them feeling abandoned or micromanaging them.

What are the resources you're spending on these people to help them grow? Do you have a development plan for each member of the team, or do you expect them to just pick up new skills on their own? Our task is to help them grow personally as well as professionally. The two spheres are always closely connected.

> You know you need ladder holders at a higher level of competence, talent, and execution if you're going to climb higher.

Do the people on your team have mentors? Are these mentors inspiring them and challenging them to grow? When was the last time you asked people on your team to describe the impact of their mentors? Mentors aren't optional because people without mentors are destined to become stagnant in their growth.

What are the choke points in your organization that block communication, stifle creativity, and create confusion and frustration? Every organization has them. What are yours? For instance, what metrics are discussed in each team meeting? Are you too focused on goals and tasks and not enough on inspiring people and creating a vibrant culture? Or are you so focused on the intangibles of the culture that people don't know what's expected of them?

How do you facilitate networking for each person on the team? Are you introducing them to outstanding leaders you've met? What books are you encouraging them to read? What conferences are you paying for them to attend? How are you helping them stay up with current trends in their roles? Who are the leaders who are forecasting change? How are you connecting your people with the most knowledgeable people in their fields?

Great leaders don't run on autopilot. They're involved in developing the people on their teams so they will be personally inspired and fulfilled, and so they will gain the skills they need for the next level of the organization's growth.

Evaluate the supervisors throughout your organization

Take time to interact individually with people at all levels of your structure, and ask a simple question: "How are you getting along with your supervisor?"

In most cases, the old saying is true: people quit their bosses, not their jobs. Some of the factors that drive employees to give up and leave are directly related to "bad bosses": overloading people with responsibilities and expecting the impossible, demanding updates on every detail of a project, failure to give adequate oversight and resources for employees to get the job done, and letting other employees poison the workplace environment.

If you don't ask, you may never know the impact of the people in leadership roles on the men and women who serve on their teams. Evaluate the influence of all the supervisors: What kind of environment are they creating? How are they providing resources, inspiration, and training? What is the mood of people several layers down the organizational chart? Ask the same questions of all your supervisors that you ask yourself.

Over-communicate and assume nothing

Too many leaders are so consumed with top-level matters that they aren't in touch with people even one layer down the organizational chart, much less the names in the boxes at the end of the lines, the men and women who connect with visitors when they walk through the doors and customers when they call to place an order.

The best leaders take time to walk the halls, stop and talk, and get to know people in the farthest offices, out in the field, and in the parking lot. These leaders understand that a personal connection takes a little time, but it may be the best investment they can make in producing a healthy organization full of people who are passionate about fulfilling the vision.

Make personal improvement plans standard operating procedure for your organization; in other words, make PIPs SOP

Personal and professional development seldom just happens. Almost always, this level of improvement is the product of intentional planning and a rigorous commitment by leaders *and* those who are being developed. This requires supervisors to become coaches who are actively involved in the lives of others instead of just telling them what to do and demanding compliance.

These four commitments help leaders close the gap between their employees' current performance and the higher level of competence they'll need for the future. It's a comprehensive process—one that promises the richest relationships, the clearest communication, and the greatest hope for real growth for each person on the team.

Quite often, especially in large organizations, I've seen top leaders who are growing quickly in their understanding, skills, and capacity, but their executive staff members don't invest time in personal and professional growth because they're so busy trying to keep up. There is a "growth gap" between the top leader and the team. The people on the team aren't thinking about increasing their capacity; they're just trying to get a million things done today! The solution is twofold: the top leaders need to invest time and resources in their executive team, and the team members need to carve time out of their packed schedules to learn and grow. Again, this isn't negotiable. It's essential if leaders are going to climb higher and if their teams are to avoid burnout.

CREATE A COLLABORATIVE ENVIRONMENT

Individual mentoring and training is important, but our efforts to equip our staff work better if people are thriving in a collaborative environment. We are social animals. Yes, plenty of people are introverts on personality profiles, but that doesn't mean they don't care about people and don't need them. It just means they gain more energy doing activities alone or with only a person or two. God has made us so that none of us can thrive without meaningful human connections. As leaders, one of our main tasks is to provide the kind of relational connections that inspire people instead of discouraging them. Let me outline a few activities leaders can use to build strong relationships on a team. In every team meeting, carve out time and be prepared to lead the team to do the following:

- *Remember and be refreshed by the grand vision* for the church, business, or nonprofit. We're thoroughly human, and it's easy to lose sight of the what and why we exist. You don't need to hand out brochures that reintroduce your people to the organization, but it would be helpful to regularly say, "Let's remember how we got to this point today," and remind people why they got up and came to the office that morning. It might not hurt you to remember it too.

> God has made us so that none of us can thrive without meaningful human connections.

- Carve out enough time to *brainstorm on important topics*. We always have more details to cover than we have time for, but great teams don't thrive on mind-numbing details. They thrive when they have time to dream, to imagine, and to bounce ideas off each other. This takes time, but it sends a loud and clear message that you value everyone's contribution.

- *Create an "iron sharpening iron" environment* (Prov. 27:17). Competition can be destructive or constructive. Envy and jealousy seriously threaten the cohesion of a team—or a marriage or any other important relationship—but good-hearted peer pressure encourages people to do their best. How can you tell the difference? It's easy. How do others respond when someone succeeds or fails? If they discount the success and glory in the failure, it's toxic. If they cheer others' success and comfort them when they fail, it's wonderfully supportive.

- Find ways to specifically complement each team member's efforts by *helping the team work collaboratively*. Stagnant and conflicted teams find ways to sabotage each other's work, but people who live and work in a supportive environment find ways to help each other accomplish their goals.

Why do people on your team come to work each day? What is it that causes the light to come into their eyes? What brings out the very best in them? Exceptional leaders and members of leadership teams don't do what they do for money, acclaim, or power. They work hard and cheerfully, facing heartaches and overcoming disasters, because they believe two incontrovertible truths: the organization gives meaning to their lives, and the people they work with are honorable people who value the same meaning. Anything less than that leads to drift, apathy, protecting turf, and the varied dark colors of fear, envy, and resentment.

> Exceptional leaders and members of leadership teams work hard and cheerfully, facing heartaches and overcoming disasters, because they believe two incontrovertible truths.

When you plan team meetings, keep these four activities in mind. Keep them in your work area so you make sure to include them in the list of topics you'll cover. Of course, you'll have to find the right balance between creating a supportive environment and covering all the details on your list—but lean toward creating the environment.

In Goethals, Roosevelt finally had the man he needed to hold his ladder. Now the new chief engineer at the canal could devote his considerable expertise to creating the systems and structures that would accomplish the mission.

THINK ABOUT THIS

Reflect on these questions and discuss them with your team:

1. If you are a senior leader, do you have the right ladder holders? How do you know? If you are a team member in charge of a major responsibility

in your organization, do you have the right ladder holders? Explain your answer.

2. If you could fire one person in your organization without fear of any consequences, do you know who it would be? If you're having a group discussion and this person is in the room, you can either be bold or pass for now. If you choose to pass, what is your plan to talk to that person or your supervisor?

3. Look back at the four parts of the process described in the section titled "A Process Before a Decision." Which of these are you doing well? Which could use some improvement? Be specific about the changes you need to implement.

4. On a scale of 0 (terrible) to 10 (awesome), rate how well you've created a collaborative environment for your team. How would your staff rate you and your team? Explain your answer.

5. Who are the star ladder holders in your organization? What are some steps you can take to celebrate them, develop others, and find new ones?

Remember: The size and speed of an organization are controlled by its systems and structures.

CHAPTER 9

HOW CAN YOU UTILIZE PEOPLE WITH DIFFERENT TALENTS?

In February 1907, George Washington Goethals arrived in Panama and evaluated the existing systems and structures at the construction site. Many of them, he realized, were efficient and effective, but some significant changes were needed. The size of the largest ships currently under construction wouldn't fit in the locks as they were currently designed. The battleship *Pennsylvania* had a beam of 98 feet and the *Titanic* was being designed at 94 feet wide, so Goethals enlarged the width of the locks from 95 feet to 110 feet.

Rock and mudslides in the Culebra Cut concerned Goethals. He realized the current plans could possibly, if not probably, result in slides that would fill the canal and close shipping for months at a time. His new plan widened the

Three Men Standing on Lock Gates
LIBRARY OF CONGRESS

bottom at the cut by half again, from two hundred to three hundred feet, which meant even more dirt and rock must be excavated from the largest earthmoving project in the world. Goethals also realized he needed to improve the port on the Pacific side to prevent silt from clogging the

entrance. These and many other changes were necessary so the canal
would remain open long after the first ship traveled from sea to sea.

To clarify the responsibilities and the reporting structure, Goethals
divided the work into three geographic regions: the Atlantic Division,
from the ocean to the locks on that side; the Pacific Division, from the
sea to the locks there; and the Central Division, consisting of everything
in between.

Perhaps the biggest change under Goethals was creating a culture of
excellence and tenacity. It was still a civilian project, but the new man in
charge was a military officer who believed in duty, honor, and country.
To Goethals, failure wasn't an option, and giving up wasn't allowed. He
appointed outstanding engineers and leaders to be responsible for every
aspect of construction in their divisions. He selected army engineers for a
few key positions, and even the civilian engineers he selected had experience working alongside army engineers on major construction projects in
the states where they had acquired the same dedication.

Three water features were used in the construction: the two oceans,
the dammed and tamed Chagres River, and an enlarged Gatun Lake that
enabled ships to have a wide area to navigate in the heart of the isthmus.

By far the greatest challenge of the project was excavating the Culebra
Cut, which was in the Central Division. For this difficult task, Goethals
chose Major David du Bose Gaillard, a man of exceptional skill. Gaillard's
executive officer wasn't an army officer. Louis Rourke had been in charge
of excavation at the Culebra Cut under Stevens, and Goethals liked what
he saw in his leadership.

The canal traveled through the forbidding landscape of high, rocky
hills near the Pacific side of the isthmus. The work at the Culebra Cut captured the public's imagination. No matter what was happening at the ports,
the dams, or the locks, the massive scar created by gigantic steam shovels at
Culebra was always on everyone's mind. Politicians and tens of thousands
of tourists traveled to Panama and took special trains to an observation
point where they marveled at the intricate and noisy work of men, shovels,
and trains. Blasts of dynamite blew holes in the rock, and steam shovels

moved thousands of tons of debris to the awaiting train cars. The trains kept rolling with amazing regularity, so the shovels never stopped.

The statistics are staggering. Sixty million pounds of dynamite were used, and 160 trains a day carried spoil to be dumped up to twenty-three miles from the Cut. Some of the dirt and rock was used to construct the dams on the Chagres River, but most of it was simply discarded at dozens of sites. The tracks had to be continually shifted to be close enough to the shovels. In a single month, March 1909, sixty-eight steam shovels removed more than two million cubic yards of rock and dirt. The total amount removed at Culebra was ninety-six million cubic yards, lowering the hills to forty feet above sea level, which is the bottom of Gatun Lake. In May 1913, the steam shovels dug down to that level—the Cut was finally finished.

The enormous locks and powerful gates were engineering marvels of their own. More than two million cubic yards of concrete were used in construction, by far the largest use of the material in a single project until twice that amount was used in the 1930s at Hoover Dam. Three sets of double locks on each side of the canal were designed to keep traffic flowing in both directions. The massive gates hold water as the level is raised and lowered. Each one is seven feet thick, and the largest weighs 662 tons.

Goethals carefully evaluated the status of the project when he arrived, kept people who proved their worth, and found new leaders who could be part of his successful team. The complexity and challenges didn't change when he took over, but he proved to be a different kind of leader: one who had a simple and clear vision and used every available resource to accomplish it.

COMPLEXITY AND DIVERSITY

Mediocre leaders gather people around them who are mirrors, reflecting only what the leader thinks, says, and does. But gifted leaders know the value—and the messiness—of complexity and diversity in their plans and their ladder holders. Goethals understood that the completion of the project required him to utilize three different water features, create three different divisions, and select three leaders whose talents and character meshed with his. The culture of any dynamic organization is rich with differing perspectives, abilities, and environments, but great leaders galvanize all of those to accomplish the single mission.

Many leaders value diversity, but they haven't clearly articulated its value to their people. Some assume diversity is skin color, ethnicity, nationality, socioeconomic status, or age—after all, those are the most visible differences among us—but real diversity is found in the multicolored hues of how people perceive and think. Our perceptions shape what we value, how we analyze challenges, how we pursue opportunities, how we relate to others, and how we communicate about all these things.

> The culture of any dynamic organization is rich with differing perspectives, abilities, and environments.

It's easy to get hung up on superficial differences and fail to tap into the insights of those who appear to be different from us. For instance, I'm a Boomer, but most of the people on my team are Millennials. I set up offices for them, but they don't go there. I outline schedules for them, but they get more done on the fly. I try to dress appropriately for people from my generation, but either they don't care about clothes or they care a lot about looking as though they don't care. If I tried to force them into my expectations, we'd both be very frustrated. We have the most productive conversations and accomplish the most when all of us realize different isn't wrong. In fact, if we look past the superficial differences, we have much more in common than we imagined.

How do we know if we're too exclusive or if we truly value diversity? It might help to think about these questions: Do we ask second and third follow-up questions to explore what people really mean, or do we quickly write them off if they don't instantly agree with us? Do we engage people on a personal level or just look at their productivity? Do we relish conversations that push our boundaries and force us to look at something from a different angle? Do we show genuine respect for others' ideas and perceptions by giving them important roles instead of busy work? Do we trust the young to add value to the older people on the team, or do the older ones dismiss their contributions?

Most of the leaders I know would insist, "I value diversity! It's not a problem at all." But when I talk to some of their young staff members, I hear a different story. The question isn't whether leaders *want* to be inclusive and *want* their teams to be diverse, but whether the people with different ideas *feel* valued. When leaders respect people on their teams, key members know it. We all have our antennae finely tuned to sense the messages that are coming to us every minute of every day. We pick up genuineness and phoniness, and young people have especially sensitive receptors.

When we choose a younger person to lead a team of older people, we need to set up the leader for success. We might tell the team, "I'm picking Sarah to lead this team. I know she's the youngest person on the team, but I think she has a unique perspective that will help you succeed. She's a little more optimistic than some of you, so listen carefully to her ideas. You'll make a great team." Our validation—our *public* validation—gives the young leader some breathing room to take the initiative.

> The question isn't whether leaders *want* to be inclusive and *want* their teams to be diverse, but whether the people with different ideas *feel* valued.

Young people are naturally optimistic and idealistic, but they can quickly turn cynical when they don't feel affirmed. When I meet with young staff members, I tell them how much I value them and their perspectives, but I also explain that I'm counting on them to take the initiative to engage and understand the older people on the team. Responsibility for good communication works both ways.

Goethals recognized the different contributions of the oceans, the river, and the lake to the completion of the canal, and he communicated the importance of these differences so the engineers in each division understood how to coordinate with each other. In the same way, leaders in churches, businesses, and nonprofit organizations need to communicate creatively, fully, and often to be sure every person on the team grasps the value of diversity in perception. Differences can be a team's greatest strength if the leader explains the power of unique contributions, or they can create silos and divisions. The leader is responsible to create a positive environment where ideas are freely shared without demanding agreement.

BLIND ADOPTION

It's inspiring to hear about the success of another church, business, or organization, but adopting another person's strategy seldom works out very well—unless the leader takes the time to understand the organizational culture where it succeeded. The idea certainly isn't wrong, but leaders need to do more spade work to uncover the underlying presuppositions where the idea was wildly successful.

> Differences can be a team's greatest strength.

For instance, the Korean church exploded to almost half of the population of the country in only a few decades. Many from the West traveled to see the phenomenon, and they watched Koreans get up in the middle of the night and trek to nearby mountains for long prayer vigils. Some pastors in the West assumed these vigils were the key to the church's growth, but when they tried them in America, they didn't see the same results. Some practices work in one culture but not in another. Programs rarely export very well, but most paradigms are universal. Even in the United States, programs that work well in the Bible Belt may not be effective in regions where fewer people regularly attend church, such as the Northeast and Northwest.

GENIUS

Goethals didn't try to force the engineering principles that worked in the ocean approaches to apply at Gatun Lake or the river, and he didn't assume what worked at Culebra was necessary in the jungles or the ports.

He carefully observed the characteristics of each part of the project and tailored his approach to each one. Goethals's genius was his ability to value the contributions of a wide variety of people and work together to make the best decisions. He minimized risks by choosing gifted and dedicated people to lead each section of the project, providing resources on time, and staying informed about the progress in all three environments and in all three divisions.

Too often, leaders subconsciously are looking for people to join their boards and hire for their teams who are just like them. They don't mean to be narrow; they just are. If we have the courage to admit our propensity to select people who consistently validate our worldview and values, we can then choose to broaden our reach and include people who may be very different from us.

For example, if a leader grew up in a home that was relatively wealthy, he may have a high risk tolerance for borrowing money for a major project. A person on his board, however, who grew up in poverty may have a very low risk tolerance. The board member's reluctance to borrow millions of dollars may seem like a lack of faith to the leader, but it's simply bringing life experiences to the table to consider in the decision-making process. Both the risk taker and the risk avoider will benefit from understanding themselves and each other. Without this understanding, negative assumptions are almost inevitable, and conflict is unavoidable. But understanding opens doors to wonderful conversations and better decisions. In fact, every decision a leader makes is a value proposition weighed against risk management.

> Every decision a leader makes is a value proposition weighed against risk management.

The leader's value of diversity is shown not only in the big decisions but also in the small ones. For instance, most leaders are verbal processors. They think best as they talk, so in a meeting they eagerly hash out ideas. They also intuitively value others who join them in the process—team members who talk with them about the concepts and plans.

But there may be a person on the team who isn't a verbal processor. In fact, this person does her best work in private when there are no distractions. If the leader doesn't grasp this trait and value it, he may quietly fume and wonder, "What's wrong with her? Doesn't she want to help us figure this out?" When the time comes to assign the project, he certainly doesn't want to give it to the person who didn't participate in the discussion. He assigns it to one of the verbal people—one he has concluded is a real team player.

The problem, though, doesn't lie with the quiet person; it's the leader's problem because he doesn't realize the value of her quiet process of analysis. She is marginalized because he doesn't understand her great strength that's so different from his. It would be much better if, in the middle of the conversation with the team, he turns to her and says, "I know you like to have time and space to think about these things. I really value your input. Would you take some time to consider all this and come back to tell me what you're thinking?" In this way, there are no "good people" and "bad people" on the team, no insiders and outsiders. All the people on the team realize they can be different and still be valued.

BROADEN YOUR CANAL

It's human nature to gravitate toward those who are like us. That's why Detroit has more Arabs than any city outside the Muslim countries, why Chicago has more people of Polish descent than any city outside Poland, and why Durban, South Africa, has more people from India than any city beyond the borders of India. Like attracts like, and even more important, compartmentalization occurs because it takes time, energy, and intention to connect with people who aren't like us. Many of us intuitively believe it's not worth the effort, but the most gifted leaders fervently believe the benefits of diversity outweigh the costs.

> All the people on the team realize they can be different and still be valued.

To achieve more size and speed, leaders need to broaden their canals. To broaden them, they need to think more expansively. To think this way, they need diverse, creative teams who stretch their minds and hearts. Change requires courage.

Leaders, go beyond what's comfortable and familiar to you. Recognize the hidden talents and perceptions of people who aren't like you. Draw them out, affirm them, and enlist their contributions. As you listen to different voices around your table, you will expand your reach, sharpen your product, and raise the quality of your services.

I know the concept of valuing diversity on your leadership team isn't new to you. You already believe it. My questions are: How well are you demonstrating that you believe it? When people look at your team, do they instantly recognize that you are a diverse group of people who work hard to blend your different perspectives for a greater good? How would a leadership consultant describe the creative diversity of your team? How does your janitor describe your team? How do people who drop in to visit describe your team? When you hire someone, do you look for someone who reflects the prevailing thoughts and perceptions, or do you try to find someone who will add a new point of view? I'm not suggesting you hire an argumentative, defiant person. Not at all. But it can be wonderfully stimulating to bring in someone who has the insight and security to offer a different perspective without insisting that everyone agree with the position.

A leader who values diversity needs more time for interaction before reaching decisions, but this type of leader's team usually comes up with better ones than homogeneous teams.

Make deliberate, conscious choices to be more diverse in the makeup of your leadership team, your board, the people on your platform, and those who represent your organization to the public. Choose diversity among the people who make initial contact with visitors or new customers.

Does your pastoral care team or HR department represent the diversity you have now or the diversity you aspire to have in the future? As you tell stories to illustrate the nature of your organization, be sure to widen the canal to include a range of characters, cultures, and concepts. Do people who come into contact with your organization conclude you're narrow or broad, insular or inclusive?

Diversity goes beyond skin color and national origin. When we have a narrow view of groups or classes of people, we tend to have clearly defined boxes with limited expectations of how "those people" think and act. But when we widen the canal, we conclude that no one has the full and final answer on how to perceive situations and how to get things done. Other people may have a new idea about systems and structures, an idea that may take us farther than we could have gone before. We can all learn from one another. We knock down the walls of the boxes and change our expectations from limited to open.

ALIGNING THE PLAYERS

Many teams in business and churches are little more than collections of individuals who come together to receive directions and give reports to the leader. A high-functioning team is very different. The leader's first task is to provide clarity about the vision: What pressing need are we meeting? How are people's lives going to be substantially better because of us? When the team is gripped with a vision to meet this kind of need, they become passionate to accomplish it. And if two or three of them aren't, it becomes obvious.

The leader's next responsibility is to enlist each person on the team to work together to craft a workable, comprehensive, cohesive plan so every aspect of the organization is dedicated to meet the need. This is the work of alignment, so that team members complement each other's efforts instead of competing. Their plans form a cohesive whole, and their hearts are in tune with one another. How does this show up? They rejoice with those who rejoice and weep with those who weep. They aren't threatened by different opinions; in fact, they relish the give-and-take of the good-hearted interchange of ideas.

As we've seen, the leader's objective is to melt and mold a diverse bunch of individuals into a group of people who trust each other, cooperate with each other, and communicate well and often with each other. They all understand the unique contribution each team member makes. They have a common purpose, a common passion, and a common strategy.

> This is the work of alignment, so that team members complement each other's efforts instead of competing.

Most leaders are somewhere in the middle of the process of creating this kind of alignment on their teams. In fact, some may have to first overcome confusion about the organization's purpose and the existing rancor among the members of the team. Misunderstandings may have grown into resentments, and these cancers must be removed so that healing can begin. It takes time to erode trust on a team, and it takes time to build or rebuild trust. But nothing can take the place of genuine respect and trust among a group of people who have a shared purpose. These traits are essential—for team alignment and for personal sanity.

Some might think diversity makes alignment harder to achieve, but the differences in outlook aren't the roadblock. The real barrier to alignment comes from suspicion and competition, no matter how homogeneous or diverse team members may be.

AMAZING OUTSIDERS

When we read the genealogy of Jesus in Matthew 1 and Luke 3, we might laugh at the surprises we find. As we read the Old Testament, we find the family history of our Lord includes plenty of misfits and outsiders—talk about diversity! Tamar and Rahab each had a checkered sexual past, Ruth was a foreigner, and Bathsheba was the woman David sent for when he was at home but should have been at war (Gen. 38; Josh. 2; Ruth 1; 2 Sam. 11). In a patriarchal culture, the listing of women in a genealogy was unusual, and the inclusion of *these* women undoubtedly shocked the first readers. And then there are the men. There are few men of honor in the list. But we also find passive Isaac, deceptive Jacob, lustful Judah, and a cast of kings that included the noble and the ignoble.

We might dismiss most of these people as too different and too flawed, but God used them in the greatest work of redemption the world has ever known—bringing Jesus Christ into the world to rescue us.

Perhaps the unlikeliest person on the list is David. When God led Samuel to Jesse's house to tap the new king, Jesse paraded his sons in front of the prophet—all but one. Jesse had such little respect for young David that he didn't even include him among his sons when one of the most important dignitaries in the nation came for a visit and specifically asked to meet his sons (1 Sam. 16).

Samuel anointed David as the new king of Israel, but David didn't insist on taking the throne. Soon King Saul's army faced the Philistines across a valley. In the rules of war, each side was to send out a champion to fight in individual combat—winner take all. The Philistines sent out Goliath, but Saul couldn't find anyone in his army to fight him. Jesse sent David to the camp of Saul's army with some groceries for his brothers who were soldiers. When David arrived and heard Goliath's taunts, the Lord stirred him and he pledged to fight the giant. Saul must have been utterly desperate to let the shepherd boy walk out on the field of battle. If Las Vegas odds makers had been around, they would have given long odds that David would be breathing a few minutes later. But a whirl of his sling and a whack of a sword ended the contest. God had accomplished his purposes through the unlikeliest of people—a young man despised by his family and not a seasoned soldier (1 Sam. 17).

God aligns himself with an incredibly diverse—and not-so-impressive—bunch of people—even people like you and me.

NOTICING PEOPLE AROUND US

I believe there are people all around us we don't even notice, or worse, we notice them but disregard them. Many of the people around us come from other cultures, have difficult backgrounds, or have checkered pasts. They may not look like us, sound like us, or think like us, but God has a purpose for them. God wants to do incredible things in them and through them, if we'll just give them the chance to serve.

How do we select people for our teams? Saul didn't have a good HR department. David was the only person willing to serve. In our organizations we need to have some criteria for selection. As we've seen, if we value diversity, we'll want people who have perspectives and backgrounds that are different from our own—not all, but at least a few. What makes them valuable? Look for men and women whose eyes light up when you talk about the need and the vision, people who have confidence in God and in themselves, and people who aren't afraid to ask hard questions and explore new ways of getting things done.

Years ago, as I was speaking on the importance of alignment, I wrote on the board: "Proper People Placement Prevents Problems." After I spoke, someone in the meeting handed me a piece of paper. It read: "Poor People Performance Prevents Prosperity." I laughed, but it's true.

Our responsibility as leaders isn't just to cast a compelling vision and then tell people what to do. Our task includes creating a diverse team of creative, insightful, passionate men and women who are dedicated to the Lord, the cause, and one another. It takes a lot of prayer, hard work, and patience, but it pays off incredibly well.

A big vision and creative people cause more disagreements than they resolve, at least at first. In the next chapter, we'll see how Roosevelt and the chief engineers used tension to accomplish the seemingly impossible.

"Proper People Placement Prevents Problems."
"Poor People Performance Prevents Prosperity."

THINK ABOUT THIS

Reflect on these questions and discuss them with your team:

1. What are some reasons diversity in perception and thinking is more important than diversity in ethnicity and skin color?
2. How do you know if you're too narrow or you truly value diversity? Rate yourself for each of these questions on a scale of 0 (not at all) to 10 (completely). Give evidence for each of your answers.
   - Do you ask second and third follow-up questions to explore what someone means?
   - Do you engage with people on a personal level or just look at their productivity?
   - Do you show genuine respect for their ideas and perceptions by giving them important roles instead of busy work?
   - Do you trust the young to add value to the older people on the team, or do the older ones dismiss their contributions?
3. Ask the people on your team to answer these questions about you. You may want to ask them to turn in their answers anonymously.
4. Where are you in the process of creating alignment on your team? Explain your answer.
5. Does the thought of having a more diverse team excite you, scare you, or annoy you? Explain your answer.

Remember: The size and speed of an organization are controlled by its systems and structures.

CHAPTER 10

HOW CAN YOU PRODUCE CREATIVE TENSION?

When Theodore Roosevelt announced his plan to complete the canal project at which the French had failed so miserably, he generated excitement, but he also created tremendous tension. American politicians and engineers suddenly had to find answers to questions that had remained unanswered since Balboa's expedition across the isthmus almost

Ship and Dredge in Culebra Cut
LIBRARY OF CONGRESS

four centuries before. Let me recount some highlights of the story, but this time I'll identify the points of tension between leaders and ladder holders, between leaders and governments, and between leaders and natural obstacles.

After Roosevelt's bold announcement, his diplomats negotiated a treaty with Colombia, but a pessimistic US Senate failed to ratify it. Undaunted by the opposition in his own government, Roosevelt suggested to Panamanian rebels that a revolution to break away from Colombia would not go unsupported.

After the quick and decisive revolution and a treaty with the new country, Roosevelt negotiated with the remnant French company to buy the existing equipment and buildings in the Canal Zone. He offered a fraction of the debt owed by the French, but they had no other options. Roosevelt's boldness and shrewd negotiating skills didn't make any friends among the French because they thought he paid too little. And in some corners of America, others thought he paid too much. Many in Congress believed Roosevelt was pursuing a fool's dream. The canal, they were sure, would never be built—in Panama or any of the other possible routes. The difficulties appeared insurmountable.

The first chief engineer, John Wallace, inherited rusting equipment, buildings that were rotting in the jungle heat and moisture, and potential workers who were understandably reluctant because they had heard horror stories of disease and death. Congress and the Isthmian Canal Commission continually got in Wallace's way.

In addition to all the engineering and political tensions, hospital wards throughout the zone filled with workers, engineers, and family members suffering from malaria and yellow fever. In all, more than fifty-six hundred died during the early years of the American effort, and Wallace was sure he would be next. Demands for progress produced tensions Wallace couldn't endure. He traveled back to Washington to meet with Secretary Taft. He offered nothing hopeful or positive, only complaints, self-pity, and doom. Taft realized Wallace's attitude had crossed the point of no return. He told him, "Mr. Wallace, I am inexpressibly disappointed not only because you have taken this step, but because you seem so utterly insensible of the significance of your conduct."

Wallace launched into a long defense of his work and reminded Taft of his many sacrifices. He told Taft that he could make much more money in another job. Taft stopped him and said bluntly, "For mere lucre you change your position overnight. . . . You are influenced solely by your personal advantage. Great fame attached to your office, but also equal responsibility, and now you desert them in an hour."

When Taft asked for his resignation, Wallace reacted, "Mr. Secretary, while there is a difference between us as to the point of view we take concerning my duty, I consider that there can be no question that I have performed my full duty up to this hour."

Taft was known as the most jovial and likable man in government, but even his patience was at an end. He answered, "Mr. Wallace, I do not consider that any man can divide such a duty up to any one point where it suits him to stop. . . . In my view a duty is an entirety, and is not fulfilled unless it is wholly fulfilled."[1]

Taft had masterfully handled the tension of unrealized expectations in Roosevelt's second most important ladder holder—Taft himself was the most important.

John Stevens understood the tension of speed and performance, and he implemented important improvements in the work. After only a year and a half, however, he was an exhausted shell of what he had been. He became paranoid about real and imagined opposition, and he found fault with everything and everyone. His complaints sounded eerily like Wallace's: the pay was too low, his family suffered by his absence, and the work was too taxing. He wrote a letter that read in part: "There has never been a day since my connection with this enterprise that I could not have gone back to the United States and occupied positions that to me, were far more satisfactory. Some of them, I would prefer to hold, if you will pardon my candor, than the Presidency of the United States."[2]

Roosevelt and Taft were not amused or persuaded. They immediately replaced Stevens with Colonel Goethals. Under Goethals's leadership at the canal, one set of tensions remained but another was resolved. All the pressures and challenges of the largest, most complicated building project in history still existed—those tensions never ceased. However, the tension between Roosevelt and his chief ladder holders was over. Similar to Taft in dedication but different in personality, Goethals poured his considerable experience and skills into the project, without complaining, without self-pity, and without delay. For seven years he coordinated the massive logistics of men and material to finish the canal.

On January 7, 1914, as the work was in the final stages of construction, the French ship *Alexandre La Valley* became the first vessel to complete the journey from sea to sea. The third form of tension—between leaders and natural obstacles—was finally overcome. On August 15, the Panama Canal officially opened with the passage of the cargo ship SS *Ancon*. All construction was finally completed and all systems functioned normally, so the Isthmian Canal Commission closed its doors. The first governor of the Canal Zone was, to no one's surprise, George Washington Goethals, now a major general in the United States Army.

EMBRACING TENSION

Throughout the world, and especially in the church, people often have misplaced expectations of life. They believe God has promised to make their lives full of peace, ease, and prosperity, and they are surprised and confused when they experience tension of any kind. Jesus told those who followed him, "Do not suppose that I have come to bring peace to the earth. I did not come to bring peace, but a sword" (Matt. 10:34). He explained that the gospel is a dividing point that can create tension in our most important relationships. In the same way, when entrepreneurs stride toward growth in business and pastors pursue the expansion of God's kingdom, tension is a predictable result.

Some might respond, "Yes, but Jesus promised peace to those who follow him." He did indeed. In John 14, he told his disciples he was granting them peace, but his version of peace, he explained, is quite different from the kind most people imagine. He told them, "Peace I leave with you; my peace I give you. I do not give to you as the world gives. Do not let your hearts be troubled and do not be afraid" (v. 27). His peace was the inner strength that enabled him to face ridicule, abandonment, and torture all the way to the cross and the tomb. Most people in our culture think of peace as the absence

> When entrepreneurs stride toward growth in business and pastors pursue the expansion of God's kingdom, tension is a predictable result.

of tension; Jesus' peace is confidence in God's presence, care, and calling in the midst of tension. That's the kind of peace we want. That's the kind we desperately need.

Many people in our organizations avoid tension at all cost and feel confused, or even betrayed by God when tension exists; *some* of our ladder holders are surprised when they encounter tension; but *all* gifted leaders have a very different perspective: their bold vision inevitably creates tension, so they expect tension, and they use tension to bring out the best in everyone around them.

All great structures have tension points built into them. Tall buildings in Los Angeles and San Francisco are engineered to withstand the shaking of earthquakes. Most bridges are made with the strongest components: concrete under compression and steel under tension. When Brenda and I celebrated our first anniversary, we drove from Portland to Seattle and had dinner at the top of the Space Needle. The wind caused the structure to sway, but it didn't collapse because the architects had built tension points into the design. When we see a tree that has fallen in a storm, we know the tension point in the trunk or underground gave way.

Tension points are the places where opposite forces are at work, where flexibility is essential, and in animate objects, where growth happens. Every physical thing in the universe has tension points, and organizations can only grow and thrive if we recognize them and use them appropriately. Trying to avoid them weakens the system and ultimately leads to a collapse—sometimes quickly and sometimes slowly.

All of us can tell stories about tension gone wrong. We've suffered shattered dreams, strained and broken relationships, and many sleepless nights. But these painful memories don't mean all tensions are destructive and need to be avoided. All great novels are about someone facing a calamity, a pivotal tension of some kind, and courageously finding a solution. If we think about it, we realize all the best stories in our own lives were written in times of the greatest threats

> Every physical thing in the universe has tension points.

we've faced. Our most cherished relationships are with people we've struggled to understand and love. Resolving the tension brought us closer together, and ongoing tension—full of honesty and authenticity—keeps the connection close. There is no such thing as a meaningful, tension-free relationship unless one of the people is dead.

I've walked into a few offices of organizations that asked me to consult with them, only to have the leaders smile and confidently tell me, "Sam, we don't have any conflict here. We live in perfect harmony with each other." They think I'll be impressed, but this statement tells me one of two things about the leader and the team: either they've all been inhaling chemicals and they're in a coma, or they have such low goals that they don't have enough passion to generate different opinions about how to get things done. If we're alive and trying to do anything significant, tension is inevitably created.

> There is no such thing as a meaningful, tension-free relationship unless one of the people is dead.

Being realistic about the value of tension brings depth to our marriages, our parenting, our friendships, our churches, our nonprofit organizations, and our businesses. Tension summons the leader's greatest efforts, deepest thoughts, and best talents. It does the same thing for our organizations and the people on our leadership teams. People are afraid of tension when they assume it will hurt them, but wise leaders use tension in ways that aren't limiting, judgmental, or condescending. They never use it to categorize or marginalize.

One of the traits of a dynamic, healthy organizational culture is that people are unafraid to share their ideas. In this environment, creative ideas flow like the waters at Niagara. But this kind of culture doesn't happen naturally. It must be modeled, cultivated, and nurtured by a leader who welcomes disagreement and doesn't insist on having the right answer or the last word. In this atmosphere, leaders can share a bigger vision for more size and speed, and the people feel the tension without being afraid.

In fact, they're inspired by the description of the pressing need and the scope of the vision to meet it.

Great leaders have always created tension and used it to inspire those around them. Martin Luther created turmoil in the church in the sixteenth century by challenging the accepted tenets and practices of Rome. He lit a fire that swept across Europe and changed history. Centuries later, his namesake, Martin Luther King Jr., refused to accept the injustice of discrimination. His eloquence and courage captured some hearts, infuriated others, and led to sweeping—if unfinished—change in our country. In every field of faith, politics, and business, entrepreneurial men and women have shaken their world, touched hearts, and galvanized the efforts of others for a great cause.

Leaders always create tension. If your intention in widening your canal is to create a tension-free zone, you can forget it. You won't create a canal that moves the masses; you'll only build a swimming pool where people relax while they do nothing.

LEADING THROUGH TENSION

The question for leaders isn't how to avoid tension, and it isn't even how to resolve tension. Resolution may seem like the highest goal, but it's not. The question is: How can you create and manage tension to bring out the best in your team? Here's another way to look at it: Can you ask the people on your team provocative questions and not be provoked when their answers are out of the box?

When I talk to leaders and know they've had an important meeting with their team or board, I ask, "How was your meeting?" Some of them respond by shaking their heads and saying, "Not too good. It was tense." I want to shout, "That's great!" but they wouldn't understand—yet.

When people say a meeting was tense,

> One of the traits of a dynamic, healthy organizational culture is that people are unafraid to share their ideas.

they often mean people got their feelings hurt, someone made statements that devalued another person, and they felt pressured to go along with a decision. No wonder people dread meetings like that!

We need to redefine "tense." When I use it to describe a meeting, I mean we had a robust exchange of ideas, people weren't afraid to voice their opinions, the culture promoted freedom of expression, disagreement was invited, decisions were made or not made as people felt heard and understood, and no one felt intimidated or overwhelmed as it all took place. People would walk out of there saying, "Man, this was fantastic!" That's the kind of tension leaders need to create and manage.

For many of us, our instant reaction to any kind of tension in the room is to fix it, smooth ruffled feathers, and find ways for people to agree. I think that's the wrong way to go. It's better to teach our people the value of tension, to tell them we welcome differing opinions, and to coach them in how to disagree agreeably. It will take time to train a team to relish tension, but it's worth the effort.

It might be necessary for the leader to admit, "People, I want us to have a different perspective on tension so we learn and grow from healthy disagreements, but I need to tell you that I've been part of the problem. I haven't felt comfortable with disagreements, so I've jumped in to resolve things too quickly. Don't get me wrong: we're not going to pummel each other. That's not healthy. But we're going to begin to value our different perspectives and become comfortable with each other as we disagree. We're going to welcome tension, learn to live with some ambiguity, disagree in ways that stimulate without harming anyone, and be as comfortable not making a decision as we are making one. It begins with me, but I want all of us to make a commitment to make tension healthy and productive on our team."

> It will take time to train a team to relish tension, but it's worth the effort.

Leaders need to assure their people of two things: "First, I'm dedicated to this change on our team; and second, I'll make any decisions that need to be made when I need to make them. I prefer for us to make most of the decisions together, but there will be a few times when I need to make them. We won't leave many things hanging, at least not for long. I value your input, but I'm still in charge. You can count on these two commitments."

The leader might also explain, "We'll probably take longer to make decisions than we have before. This may frustrate some of you—and it may frustrate me sometimes. But I don't want to short-circuit the process of getting your best ideas, and that takes time. If we take a little more time, you will sometimes say one sentence that takes us in a direction we never dreamed of going—a really good direction. And as we learn to live in this creative tension, our relationships with each other will grow because we'll understand each other better than ever."

We often hear leaders and team members insist, "We need to be on the same page." In the church world, we might point to the passage in Amos: "Do two walk together unless they have agreed to do so?" (Amos 3:3). The implication is that disagreement is somehow sub-Christian and ungodly, to be avoided by saying yes even when we mean no. I don't think that's what the passage means at all. Two people can agree to walk together in a commitment to the health and strength of the relationship even if they don't agree about every topic. Their commitment is to communicate clearly, believe the best of each other, and avoid making mountains out of molehills. Their relationship is far stronger if they can disagree about something without ridicule, running away, or acting as though it doesn't matter. Their commitment to one another enables them to disagree without harming the relationship. They can be on the same page even if they're writing different content.

If we insist on having our way, and if we insist that we're right, we won't be able to disagree without hurting the people around us. We'll perceive every challenge as a threat instead of an invitation to explore another point of view. With stability, security, and wisdom, we can love those who disagree with us, we can listen carefully to them with an open heart and without defensiveness, and in most cases we can support the person responsible for making the decision even if we would have made a different one. Of course, if the decision is a watershed of ethics and morality or a central issue of the faith, we can love and listen but we can't support the other view. In those cases, we need to be very clear about our position so there's no misunderstanding.

Everything doesn't need to be tied up in a bow at the end of a team meeting. Certainly, some things need to be finalized and resolved, but sometimes it's best to let things hang—to ask people to think about a topic and live with ambiguity for another week. Even then, everyone doesn't have to agree, but the goal is for everyone to feel heard.

Leaders generate tension to bring out the best in their team, but they also experience tension in many other realms: with the bank, the builder, vendors, the worship leader, the denomination, the board, the budget, the top donors, community leaders, and many others. Leaders experience tension in the sequencing of events on the way to fulfill the vision as people prioritize different components. Every hire is a moment of tension to match the needs of the organization with the qualifications of the applicant, and the decision is never a sure thing. Leaders find inherent tensions in every decision related to growth: the height of the ladder, the speed of expansion, the focus of outreach, and the people to lead these efforts.

> The goal is for everyone to feel heard.

We need to teach our teams that the decision-making apparatus needs to be respected. Some decisions may be made by a vote, others by consensus, and still others by the person in charge. Whatever the case, the entire team owns the decision. This means we welcome disagreement and the free exchange of ideas within the team, but when the responsible person makes a decision, everyone supports it to those outside the team. They don't nod at the end of the meeting and then walk out and tell a friend how dumb the decision is.

The ability to embrace and use tension is one of the biggest tools in the leader's toolbox to widen the canal to provide more size and speed for the organization. Tension is an enemy only if we are afraid of it and we let it poison relationships. If we teach our people the benefits of creative disagreement, we'll stimulate creativity and uncover more opportunities. It's well worth the time and effort.

CRAFT GREAT MEETINGS

Do you view staff meetings as a necessary evil or the best part of your week? Do your people dread them because they are bored or feel devalued, or do they look forward to them because they know they'll contribute in meaningful ways? Do they understand that you welcome healthy tension, or are they afraid to voice an opinion?

We walk into meetings with the goal of coming out with good decisions and a commitment on the part of everyone to do everything possible to make it work, but most leaders need a few reminders of what makes a great meeting. Leadership guru Peter Drucker observed, "The understanding that underlies the right decision grows out of the clash and conflict of opinions and out of the serious consideration of competing alternatives."[3] Let me offer a few suggestions and ideas to craft meetings you and your team won't want to miss.

- *Take the pressure off.* There's no need to stimulate creativity—just release the creativity inherent in each person. God has made every person with a spark of creativity. It's part of the *imago dei*, the image of God in each of us. Some show this trait by challenging assumptions, but others demonstrate creativity by looking for new alternatives. It's not that one is bad and the other is good. Both are essential and need to be celebrated.
- *Start well.* In your planning, consider what will make people glad to be together. You might have good news to share, or you might ask about a personal victory or struggle. Whatever it is, create a positive connection from the outset.
- *Regularly go back to the need and the vision.* Passion drifts, so reinforce the why and the what so people on your team have context for the how, who, and when.

- *Have a shorter time for reports and more time for questions, ideas, and connections to other departments* so the team feels like a cohesive whole instead of a bunch of isolated managers.
- *Separate identity from ideas.* A dumb idea doesn't mean the person is dumb. Be careful to avoid verbal snickers and nonverbal sneers. All people have inherent value, even if their ideas don't make the cut.
- *Value the team.* People instinctively want to receive credit and avoid blame. Pride and fear won't be eradicated on this side of heaven, but we can continually remind people that everyone on the team plays a valuable part in every decision.
- *Enlist everyone's input.* It's easy to let the talkers dominate discussions, but don't let the others be overlooked. They often have thoughtful, creative ideas, and they need to be invited to the conversation.
- *Value your instincts as a leader,* but don't play the "Trust me on this one" card too often. You need a full tank of trust to draw on anytime you ask your people to trust you when they see things differently. If you draw it down too often, you run the risk of losing everyone but those who are blindly loyal—and that's its own kind of problem.
- *Constraint stimulates creativity.* We've said that the early planning process needs to be unhurried so everyone can contribute, but later, it's time to finalize plans and get moving. In the later stages of planning, don't be afraid of time pressures to make decisions. In many cases a little pressure causes adrenaline to flow a bit more and sharpens the focus of thinking.
- *End on a high note.* In your planning, don't let meetings end with people rushing out the door. Plan the ending as well as you plan the beginning, and make it meaningful and uplifting.

Everywhere Roosevelt went, he shook things up. He created tension with his bold vision for the Panama Canal, for national parks, breaking up massive companies that were dominating the markets and limiting competition, and many other endeavors. He wasn't afraid of disagreement, and he wasn't shy about expecting the best from those on his team. As we widen our canals, tension is inevitable. Learn to use it for good.

Under Roosevelt, Taft, and Goethals, the Panama Canal was completed in 1914—ten long years after Americans arrived on the isthmus. It was a monumental success that made shipping much more affordable, but like every major project that stays in operation for a long time, it needed constant management and periodic upgrades. In the next chapter, we'll look at the work at the canal in the decades that followed its opening.

THINK ABOUT THIS

Reflect on these questions and discuss them with your team:

1. What are some indications in our culture and our organizations that some people expect perfect peace instead of tension?
2. What are some reasons people are afraid of tension? Which of these are understandable? Which are unreasonable? Explain your answer.
3. In the past when you've described a meeting as "tense," what have you meant? How does the definition in this chapter change your concept of tension in a meeting?
4. Write a plan for how you'll teach and train your team to view healthy disagreement as a necessary part of your interactions.
5. Look at the suggestions about crafting stimulating meetings. Which three seem most important to implement soon? How will you make them happen?

Remember: The size and speed of an organization are controlled by its systems and structures.

CHAPTER 11

DOES IT EVER END?

The canal operated beautifully after it was opened—ten long years after Americans arrived on the isthmus—but it required constant maintenance. Heavy rains caused minor mudslides, and silt filled the bottom of Gatun Lake, the locks, and the approaches on both sides of the isthmus. Dredges were constantly busy clearing the bottom so ships with deep drafts could pass easily. The engines that opened the gates at the locks needed continuous maintenance to be sure the gates opened smoothly and completely, assuring the flow of traffic would not be impeded.

In the 1930s, periods of floods and droughts proved to be a problem. Water flowing from the Chagres River into the canal needed to be regulated more completely, so a new dam was constructed to create Madden Lake as another reservoir for the canal's need for plenty of water. By late in

Gatun Locks with Tugs, Dredges, and Barges
LIBRARY OF CONGRESS

the decade, tensions were rising in Europe and Asia. Germany was rearming and building the largest battleships on the seas, and Japan had already invaded Manchuria and China. They, too, were building larger battleships than had ever been seen before.

The United States had no intention of entering a war on either continent, but the navy didn't want to be in trouble if they were forced into combat. They made plans to build a larger fleet of Montana-class battleships, ones that wouldn't fit into the locks in Panama. To accommodate the size of these ships, the locks had to be widened. Soon after work began, the Japanese bombed Pearl Harbor, and the United States entered the war. The authorities realized the new locks wouldn't be completed for six years, so the larger ships would continue to travel the long route around Cape Horn. The commanders determined this was too long to wait, so the project was shelved and work stopped. Still, regular maintenance to keep the canal operating smoothly remained a high priority.

In 1954, Egypt's General Nasser led an attack on the British forces controlling the Suez Canal. The successful takeover of the Suez prompted demands from Panama for the United States to relinquish control of the Canal Zone. The demands grew over the next few years, culminating in riots in January 1964, costing the lives of several US soldiers and twenty Panamanians.

In 1977, President Jimmy Carter negotiated a new treaty with Panama, giving up control of the canal in exchange for a guarantee of neutrality by the Panamanian government. On the last day of the century, the Panama Canal Authority took control of the Canal Zone. From that point, scheduling the ships in the canal and performing routine maintenance were Panama's responsibility.

Throughout its history, the canal has required a substantial workforce. As many as forty-five thousand were employed during the peak years of excavation and construction, and today, about nine thousand people manage the operations at the canal. For more than a hundred years, the complex and massive operation has required constant attention. Engineers must anticipate needs before they exist and marshal resources to fix problems before they happen.

NO COASTING

Some emerging leaders believe that if they can ever achieve their grand plan for growth, they can then hit the autopilot button and coast to ever-higher levels of size and speed. Wiser leaders know it doesn't work that way. When they hit their highest goals, they certainly celebrate, and they may take a few days to relax, but they're soon back at the job because their work never ends. They realize Point B on the Sigmoid Curve (described in chapter 3) is always on the horizon. The forces of entropy, the tendency toward disorder, operate in every sphere in nature, and they operate in organizations too. If we're not diligent, things will begin to unravel—sometimes with alarming speed.

Leaders work with their people to produce excellent programs. Plans and projects are like landscapes: growth comes in seasons over longer periods of time, but devastation can occur quickly in storms or gradually in droughts. People are like seascapes: constantly changing with the storms and tides.

Many leaders strive for stability and consistency, but I would argue that these aren't the right goals. Too often they lead to stagnation and eventual erosion. In seasons of an organization when we consolidate growth, we need to be vigilant to keep the operation running smoothly. Our commitment is always to excellence. Then, when the time is right, we will be ready to launch the next new initiative.

> People are like seascapes: constantly changing with the storms and tides.

I've talked to many leaders who were frustrated that people on their teams weren't as compliant and eager to help as they expected. They had come to the conclusion that their people were deficient, lazy, and selfish, and these leaders felt tired, unappreciated, and beleaguered. Their chief goal was stability. I saw it as a leadership problem. In a thousand small increments, these leaders had interpreted questions as resistance and delays as defiance. After a while, they believed their people were against them. If that's true, it's usually because the team members don't feel valued and inspired. At that point, pep talks are counter-productive because those on the team feel manipulated. It's like putting a coat of paint on a rotting piece of wood. It doesn't do anything for the underlying problem: a lack of trust.

As all this unfolds, the leader's vision deteriorates. It's like silt building up in the approaches, the lake, and the locks of the canal, gradually clogging the channel and impeding progress. Instead of dreaming about substantial growth, the goal for embattled leaders is to stop the silt from getting even deeper. They just try to get through staff meetings without frustrated people blowing up or bored people looking at their phones a dozen times. These are signs erosion has already set in.

The supreme yearning for stability is a sign of a stagnant organization, and perhaps toxicity. It never leads to growth. It doesn't stimulate new ideas, it doesn't challenge the status quo, it doesn't inspire anyone, and it doesn't force people to find ways to work together to fulfill a goal no one can accomplish alone. Leaders who become stagnant are defensive and react against every challenge. They hire people primarily for personal loyalty rather than finding people who will add spice to the mix. They look for team members who are supportive and compassionate like John, the beloved disciple, rather than looking for people like Peter, who was brilliant but impulsive, or Paul, who was a lightning rod wherever he went.

Leaders need to continually dredge their organization's canal to be sure nothing blocks the flow of energy and ideas, and they need to keep a sharp eye on the machinery, the systems, to be sure they function smoothly. Silt and rust were constant threats in the Panama Canal after it opened, and leaders face similar challenges after they've reached milestones of growth.

The supreme yearning for stability is a sign of a stagnant organization, and perhaps toxicity.

Team cohesion and congruence can't happen unless the individuals on the team are growing and excited.

Sometimes if only one person is ignited by a new passion to accomplish a grand goal, the enthusiasm can spread to others on the team. The pursuit of stability is a hindrance; all growth is pregnant with change, and change is inherently unstable.

But leaders need to set some boundaries about the creativity they invite from their staff. Members of the team need to communicate with respect and patience, not with demands. As trust grows, the leader and those on the team will learn to value one another and stimulate one another to excel.

Suspicion, hurt feelings, and misguided expectations are other layers of silt that block our canals. We can't completely stop them from happening. They're part of being human and part of being on a team, but leaders can notice these things as they happen and deal with them clearly and gracefully. Team members need to be willing to listen, forgive, and keep working with each other. This effort is like the regular maintenance of the Panama Canal. Our canals won't work well if we don't dredge the channel regularly and oil the organizational machinery.

> Our canals won't work well if we don't dredge the channel regularly and oil the organizational machinery.

Like Roosevelt, all great leaders are dreamers, and like him, great leaders find people who share their dreams and become deeply committed to making them happen. When they encounter people with passion but limited skills, they find a place somewhere for them to serve faithfully and well. When they find people with skills but no passion, they try to inspire commitment and zeal for the cause—and if the people don't respond, the leaders replace them. But people with great ideas never threaten gifted leaders. These leaders regularly stir the pot, and they appreciate others who stir it too.

Big ideas—and even the accomplishment of those dreams—must be followed by the day-to-day maintenance of the systems and structures so the organization continues to fulfill its mission. Leaders need outstanding ladder holders at every stage of organizational growth.

CYCLES

Vibrant organizations go through cycles of intense creativity and maximum effort, followed by times when the gains are consolidated. In the periods of consolidation, new leaders who join our organizations must be trained so they can become effective for the next cycle of growth. We need to stop often to reflect on what God has done and on the faithfulness of men and women who have contributed so much to the cause, and we give thanks. Gratitude is never out of season. It reminds all of us who we depend on, who is the source of our growth and joy, and who we trust for the future.

We can certainly have stability in the faces at the table when we meet with our teams, but we expect those people to be growing, changing, and reaching higher. They sharpen their existing skills and uncover new talents. They learn how to enlist, place, and motivate people more effectively, and they have a bigger view of what God might do through them. They ask hard questions about the existing systems and structure, knowing that these will change as they reach for more size and speed. In this way team members stimulate one another, pushing and pulling others to dream bigger dreams and find better ways to fulfill them. They're constantly gaining new skills, and they're regularly refining the mechanisms that keep the system going.

> Gratitude is never out of season.

Leaders can help their teams by describing the normal cycle of growth in any organization and then pinpointing their current position on the cycle. They might use the Sigmoid Curve, or they can use the five stages we describe in chapter 1: entrepreneurial, emerging, established, eroding, and enterprising. In this way people on the team will realize when it's time to launch new plans and when it's time to consolidate gains.

Good leaders also provide helpful guidelines. One business leader told an eager department head, "Don't bring a $10 million idea if you only have a $1 million budget." At every point in the cycle, team members should give input and feedback with honor and respect, and they need to learn to avoid using a negative comparison to another's idea in promoting their own. If an idea isn't clear, instead of shooting the idea down, the leader can teach people on the team to say, "Help me understand what you're saying." Certainly, the leader's patience will be a good model for the rest of the team.

We don't build trust by insisting on unanimity and instant compliance, but by valuing the input of every person on the team and providing time—within limits—for people to push back and give input. This is the kind of environment that stimulates the next wave of ideas that lead to creativity, energy, and growth.

If the Panama Canal Commission had folded their hands and said, "Our job is done" when the canal opened in 1914, the lake and locks would have soon filled with silt, so only shallow draft boats could use it. And sometime later, the engines opening and closing the enormous gates at the locks would have ground to a halt, and the canal

> We don't build trust by insisting on unanimity and instant compliance, but by valuing the input of every person on the team.

wouldn't have been usable for any boats or ships. For those in charge of the canal, the work was never finished. The spectacular work of digging the Culebra Cut—renamed the Galliard Cut in honor of Major Galliard, who was instrumental in the years of digging at the site—and building the locks and gates was finally done, but continual maintenance was essential for the canal to keep functioning.

THE CONTINUAL TASK

Do businesses need to produce and market excellent products to capture the market? Yes, of course. Do nonprofits need a compelling mission to raise money and provide resources to the poor and needy? Certainly. Do churches need excellent teaching and preaching, as well as inspiring worship? Undoubtedly. But in my experience consulting with leaders in businesses, nonprofit organizations, and churches, I can confidently say that the single factor that has led to growth is consistent and effective leadership development.

Too often management teams focus on the brilliance of a single leader or they continue to use a strategy that worked incredibly well in the past. If they have this kind of myopia, they fail to see what makes their organizations hum. The principles are the same in any field, from manufacturing to missions, from restaurants to churches. Let me use the church as an illustration. We might view the relationships around and in the church in concentric circles:[1]

The church needs to have a vibrant presence in the community—not just a building in the community. The church is most powerful when its people

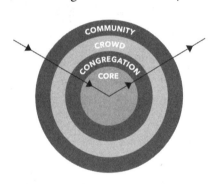

are woven into the fabric of the community: loving, serving, and caring in schools, businesses, government, sports activities, and touching those in need.

Some of the people in neighborhoods, schools, offices, and shops will be attracted by something in the church: the personal connection of love from those who attend, the selfless service they see in everyday life, or the way the church meets needs in times of crisis. Some of them come to check out what's going on at the church. A friend may have invited them, or they may just drop in because they heard this was a different kind of church. Those who stay become part of the congregation by attending faithfully and giving to the ministry of the church.

The church's leaders often use the number of people in the congregation as the primary benchmark of success, along with the size of the buildings and the cash in the bank account. But the true mark of success is the size and strength of the core of leaders who shoulder the burden and spread the joy of God throughout the ministry of the church.

If we look at the life of Jesus, we see these concentric circles of relationships. At times, it appears the whole countryside came to hear him. The Gospels record the miracle of Jesus turning a boy's lunch into a feast for five thousand men, and probably twenty thousand people including women and children.[2] And we get glimpses of crowds who pressed in to hear him teach and see him heal the sick. His "congregation" appears to be the seventy he sent out to preach about the kingdom, heal the sick, and cast out demons. But the core of Jesus' ministry, the ones he spent the most time preparing, were the twelve disciples. Of the twelve, Jesus often called three to be his closest confidants: Peter, James, and John. Even his core had a core.

In our churches the core consists of our volunteers, the people who have demonstrated a high level of commitment to Christ and his cause. The staff's main responsibility is to attract, recruit, place, train, and nurture as many volunteers as possible. I've noticed that the focus on volunteers is central to the strategy of some churches, but it's an afterthought to others. I look at the ratio of church attendance to the volunteers who serve. If we evaluate a handful of churches, we see the differences:

There is no magic percentage that guarantees success in developing leaders, but anything higher than a 5:1 ratio probably means the leaders of the church are relying too heavily on the pastor's eloquence, a beautiful building, or a few outstanding programs to attract and keep people in the circle of the congregation.

In a survey of leadership teams in hundreds of churches around the country, the Vanderbloemen Search Group and the Unstuck Group identified three practices that had the biggest impact on developing a strong core of leaders:

> The [church] staff's main responsibility is to attract, recruit, place, train, and nurture as many volunteers as possible.

- an intentional strategy of leadership development
- a significant financial investment in staff development
- a specific person who is responsible for developing leaders

#	SUNDAY ATTENDANCE	VOLUNTEERS (LEADERS, PEOPLE, ETC)	RATIO
1	1500	300	5
2	750	100	7.5
3	2400	800	3
4	1200	120	10

The average growth rate for churches that implement all three practices was found to be 22 percent. The growth rate for churches that implement two of them is roughly one-third that: 8 percent. But only 11 percent of the churches in the survey implement all three practices. More than seven in ten churches invest in staff development, but only 19 percent of churches have a strategy to develop leaders in their congregations.[3]

Leadership development doesn't just happen. Organizations need a comprehensive plan to expand the number of people in the core and sharpen their skills and effectiveness. This plan can't be an add-on; it must become central to the strategy. Many people have described a "leadership pipeline," with a wide opening to invite people in the congregation to sign up as volunteers; and then, with training, mentoring, and involvement, those who are involved find the place where they want to serve—a place where opportunity, capacity, skill, and passion converge. Along the way, people may try many different ministries. Most people find the place where they fit best only after a season of experimentation.

The same principles apply with the development of employees in a business. The company has more invested in new hires than churches have in new volunteers, so the HR department screens applicants more rigorously than churches screen those who show up to serve. But the best companies have the same three practices in place to identify rising leaders, develop them, and place them where they can be most effective for the company.

> Leadership development doesn't just happen.

When I talk to leaders and ask them for their growth goals, many look surprised by my question and say, "To grow as big and as fast as we can." I encourage them to be more specific. There are, of course, many factors that determine the size and speed of growth, but leaders can at least have a specific target they're shooting for. The target then shapes their plans to sharpen their systems and structures. In every aspect of the organization, they can identify a target and a timeline: X percentage of growth in Y length of time. For instance, one pastor came back with these specific goals:

The numbers and times in this chart aren't a rigid formula for success. The point isn't to use these goals or ratios, but to have your own specific targets. This chart illustrates the kind of conversations for leadership teams to have as they set visionary goals and timetables.

Worship	From 400 to 600	In two years
Students	From 75 to 150	In two years
Summer missions	From 25 to 100	Next year
Women's Ministry	From 75 to 120	In one year
Men's Ministry	From 50 to 75	In one year
Volunteers	From 80 to 150	In two years

From my perspective, the pastor's most important target is for volunteers. In fact, each of the areas of ministry needs a target for volunteers. The quantity and quality of these people are often the most significant factors in reaching each ministry's specific targets. Weekly reports, staff evaluations, and periodic celebrations shift from sheer numbers to the percentage growth in the core of committed, trained, and passionate volunteers. That's how the goals will be reached.

In staff meetings, the leadership pipeline becomes one of the consistent topics of conversation. In many ways, it is the primary way each staff member in a business or church—and each key volunteer in smaller churches—learns to view his or her responsibilities. If leadership development isn't progressing, something needs to change.

A common misconception is that leadership training occurs in classes. In fact, knowledge can be imparted in classes, but training happens in the field as people are exposed to real-life situations and coached by someone who sees potential, accelerates growth, and helps people overcome confusion, difficulties, and failure. Again, the life of Jesus is our model for leadership development. From the crowd of interested people who followed him, he chose twelve and poured his life into them. It appears other men and women were part of this troop that traveled throughout Galilee, Samaria, and Judea, but Jesus focused on the twelve. He taught them as they walked along the dusty roads and around countless campfires and in homes, but none of this was sterile. He explained what they had seen him do, and he explained what they were going to see him do. He used common, everyday themes in the culture to illustrate his points. After they watched him teach thousands, he often took them away so they could talk about what they'd experienced.

Jesus was incredibly patient and kind, but he wasn't shy about putting his followers in challenging situations. He sent them out in pairs to do what they had seen him doing. Later, they realized they were in danger because the authorities considered Jesus a revolutionary. If they wanted to kill him, they certainly would kill them!

> A common misconception is that leadership training occurs in classes.

Jesus was the greatest leader in the history of the world. His followers now number more than two billion scattered throughout the earth, but he didn't leave them a comprehensive manual and a checklist to follow. He left them a mandate we call the Great Commission, which I call "the Great Assignment." His mandate to his followers is both exceedingly broad and very specific. Before he ascended, he told them, "All authority in heaven and on earth has been given to me. Therefore go and make disciples of all nations, baptizing them in the name of the Father and of the Son and of the Holy Spirit, and teaching them to obey everything I have commanded you. And surely I am with you always, to the very end of the age" (Matt. 28:18–20).

The mission is to make disciples of all nations. It can't get any bigger than that! How? By baptizing those who believe and teaching them. What would they teach and how would they teach it? The remaining disciples were tasked with following the model of Jesus: to impart truth and grace in the context of strong relationships in every conceivable situation. The task is monumental and the strategy is comprehensive, but we aren't alone. Jesus, the one who has full authority "in heaven and on earth," is with us by the presence and power of the Holy Spirit. Leadership development was the central ministry strategy of Jesus Christ. His message and his heart have spread throughout the world, starting with a handful of people who, at first glance, wouldn't have been considered "most likely to succeed" among those watching them that fateful day. But Jesus had prepared them, and, with his power and love, they changed the world.

> Leadership development is the way healthy organizations maintain the growth they've realized, and it's how they continue to grow.

Great leaders come from a hothouse of growth, where the gospel message, motivations, and methods are modeled and imparted by loving, talented men and women. Leadership development is the way healthy organizations maintain the growth they've realized, and it's how they continue to grow.

Sometimes leaders need to inject a fresh vision into the life of the organization to jump-start a new wave of growth. The completion of a project or the fulfillment of a goal gives leaders and their teams the confidence to try something new—to inject a new wave of instability into the organization. New ideas and bigger visions aren't seen as threats but as the next wave in a never-ending pursuit of *what might be* instead of settling for *what already is*. New products are envisioned, new groups to be reached are identified, new strategies are considered, and new leaders are enlisted.

After almost a century of continuous use, the Panama Canal needed to be enlarged to accommodate much larger modern ships.

THINK ABOUT THIS

Reflect on these questions and discuss them with your team:

1. When did you realize that meeting your primary goal wasn't the end of your own growth and the growth of your organization? How did you handle that reality?
2. When is the longing for stability unhealthy?
3. On a scale of 0 (nonexistent) to 10 (exceptional), rate your organization in your implementation of the three practices of leadership development. Explain your answer to each one:
   - an intentional strategy of leadership development
   - a significant financial investment in staff development
   - a specific person who is responsible for developing leaders

4. How does—or how would—having specific targets and timelines for growth in each area of your organization help your team focus your energies and develop leaders?
5. Describe how Jesus developed leaders. How does this compare with the strategy of leadership development in your organization?

Remember: The size and speed of an organization are controlled by its systems and structures.

CHAPTER 12

WHAT'S THE NEXT BIG DREAM?

When the nation of Panama took control of the canal on the last day of 1999, the newly formed Panama Canal Authority faced a serious problem. In recent years nations had been building larger cargo ships that couldn't fit in the locks of the canal, so they were losing business. The aborted effort to expand the locks before World War II was a distant memory, but it was time to revive the idea. Panama held a referendum in 2006, and 76 percent of voters approved a budget of $5.25 billion.

Companies were invited to submit designs and budgets for the authority to consider. A year later, though, a geologist issued a report that Panama's risk for earthquakes of up to 8.0—a devastating quake—was much higher than previously predicted. Still, three consortiums of builders prepared bids to complete the work.

After more than a year of planning and negotiations, the three groups submitted their offers, including one led by Bechtel, one of the largest and most respected building contractors in the world. One of the groups, however, was considered bankrupt and out of the running. In July 2009, it was announced that the consortium with the weakest financial backing, the one others had written off as totally unprepared and unacceptable, had been selected. The bid was $3.2 billion, a billion less than the next lowest offer.

Construction began on new locks that were designed to be 1,400 feet long, 400 feet longer than the ones that had been used for almost a century. The new locks were designed to be 180 feet wide instead of 110 feet. However, tugboats instead of railway engines (or "mules") were to move the ships. The tugs would take up space in the locks, so the largest ships that would fit would be 1,200 feet long. Still, the new locks provided for ships with a capacity more than two and a half times larger than before. While the largest of the ships that previously fit in the locks were called Panamax ships, the new larger size specifications now allow for what are called Neopanamax ships.

Construction proved to be problematic. A leak in one of the new Pacific locks threatened to stop work. The engineers considered two options: tearing out the locks and rebuilding them or reinforcing them with steel. They chose the cheaper and quicker method of reinforcement. The authority bought fourteen specially designed tugs from Spain, but they were unstable and performed well only when going backward, which was impossible in the locks. There was more than a hint of corruption in the decision to purchase the tugs. It was later discovered that the canal authority spent $158 million to buy tugboats from a company represented by the canal administrator's son.

By the time construction was finished almost two years behind schedule, the builder had run up more than $3.4 billion in additional costs—a figure more than the original bid. Some tug pilots claimed the canal was relatively safe when winds were calm but dangerous under windy conditions.

On June 9, 2016, the first Neopanamax ship entered the new locks on the Atlantic side of the canal. The official opening was two weeks away, but the authority wanted to be sure the new locks were operational. Only weeks after the opening, one of the first ships to make the passage, a Chinese container ship named *Xin Fei Zhou*, struck a wall, gashing the hull. The ship was out of service until it could be repaired, at a cost of several hundred thousand dollars, approximately the amount the shipping company saved by using the canal. Officials at the canal claimed the damage was minor and insisted the new locks were safe.

An additional problem surfaced because the larger ships have a deeper draft, requiring deeper locks and channels. During a drought, the river system didn't have enough water to adequately supply the canal, so some of the largest ships had to lighten their loads to make it through. Progress at the canal came with plenty of setbacks, but it was progress nonetheless.

The redesigned Panama Canal has created ripple effects at ports around the world, and especially on the American coasts. Some railroads have had to anticipate less cargo as the cost of shipping through the canal has made ocean shipping more competitive. Not long after the expansion project was completed, officials at ports on the West Coast were hopeful they could maintain their current volume, but ports on the Atlantic and the Gulf Coast expected a potential bonanza. In the years after the new locks became operational, Savannah, Georgia, planned to invest more than $700 million in expanding its port facilities to handle larger ships, and New York is in the process of raising the Bayonne Bridge so the big ships can pass beneath the roadway. Farm products and natural gas from the Midwest can now flow from Gulf Coast ports through the canal to destinations in Asia.

The people of Panama are counting on the new and improved canal to bolster their economy. They made a big bet on the success of expansion. So far, shippers are lining up to make the transit with larger ships. The true impact of the new construction won't be fully known for a few years, but the canal will continue to play an enormous role in the world's transportation of commerce and military resources.

WHAT'S NEXT?

Why do some leaders wait so long to launch a new wave of growth? There may be many reasons. Some simply don't realize their organizations are eroding in front of their eyes, others are afraid of the pushback they'll undoubtedly feel if they launch a new initiative, and a few are simply exhausted and lack the energy to lead the charge. Whatever the reason, these leaders and their organizations miss the opportunity to increase their size and speed because they fail to revitalize their systems and structures.

Why do some leaders wait so long to launch a new wave of growth?

We might look at the recent expansion of the Panama Canal and conclude these leaders waited too long. Shipbuilders had been constructing larger ships for years— ships that couldn't get through the canal. Few of them made the voyage around the tip of South America into another ocean, so they were relegated to transverse the Atlantic or the Pacific. If we said the Panama Canal Authority waited too long, these officials would answer that they didn't have control of the zone until 1999, and at that point they moved as quickly as they could with the massive project. There are always reasons and excuses to avoid launching bold, new projects. Great leaders like Theodore Roosevelt find ways to move ahead despite them.

Are true leaders ever satisfied? Is a certain level of size and speed enough? Are there no more mountains to climb and no new lands to discover? Is incremental growth acceptable, or is it time to launch something that will propel the organization to a higher level?

KEY QUESTIONS

If you are a leader, you may be thinking about a new product, a new market, a new building, or a new strategy, but you haven't told anyone about it yet. So far the idea has been vague, but it's taking shape. You're in the pre-contemplation phase of planning. You're excited about the possibilities, but you're scared it won't work and people will think you've lost your mind. Within minutes you blow hot and cold on the idea. You wake up in the middle of the night with new ideas of how it might work, but you also wake up in cold sweats because it may cost you everything. You don't know who you can trust with your secret, but you can't hold it in much longer.

Let me suggest a few questions to consider:

- Is the new idea a fine-tuning of the current plan, or is it a drastic leap?
- Can you accomplish the same objective by going slowly, or can the

goal only be fulfilled by being bold? In other words, is the timeline the only real variable?

- Who is the best person who will listen carefully and give you wise feedback? Find someone who doesn't have a stake in the decision and can be totally objective—not a friend who will tell you what he thinks you want to hear.
- How will this person help you gather your scattered and conflicting thoughts so they become more cogent?
- What is the real objective? What will this new idea achieve? What pressing need will it meet? A new product, sales target, building, or program isn't the real objective. These are means, not ends. For nonprofit organizations, the real objective may be to provide resources to people who are in desperate need. Churches want to reach unreached people, be Christ's hands and feet to touch those in need, and have a profound impact on the community. Businesses want to raise the share price, increase market share, build credibility in the market, raise the company's credit rating, and provide profits for shareholders.
- Do you have enough gas in the tank to see the plan to completion? And do you have enough bandwidth to pour time and energy into this project? If not, is there someone who can pick up the baton and carry it across the finish line? David brought the ark of the covenant back to Jerusalem, but his son Solomon built the temple, the permanent house of God (2 Sam. 6; 1 Kings 6).
- Do you have enough emotional margin to handle the resistance and ridicule? Do you have enough psychological strength to deal with your own self-doubts and second-guessing?
- Will the primary stakeholders get behind this effort? Every major project has one major requirement—and it's not money; it's the support and involvement of key people. They may be board members or venture capitalists who are willing to take a risk with you. If they believe in you and your vision, their money will follow.
- All major efforts come at a cost. What will it cost you? What will

you have to give up to make this happen? If you think you can add a new venture to your existing responsibilities and schedule, mediocrity and failure are right around the corner.

- Do you need to cast the new vision to create enthusiasm for building the new systems and structures to complete it, or do you need to carefully craft the systems and structures first before you announce the new initiative? Many leaders assume the vision must come first, but it's a very strong position to be able to announce that the systems and structures are in place.

The stakeholders always want to see more specifics than the grand idea of a vision. They insist on understanding how the plan will be achieved. They intuitively ask, "Can you really do this? Are you ready?" Their questions about readiness point to the systems and structures that already have been put in place or are being put in place. They ask the same questions I've listed for leaders to ask themselves. You may have a vision for an enormous Airbus 380 that holds as many as 853 passengers, but your stakeholders want to know how you'll build the runway and gates for it. It's more impressive if you can show them the runway is already built or at least far along under construction.

Before articulating the vision, anticipate the stakeholders' questions. If you can answer their questions, objections will be reduced to a minimum. It would be wise to be able to tell them something like this: "Here's a new venture for size and speed, and the good news is that we already have the systems and structures in place to achieve it. Our team has been working hard for the last eighteen months to get ready for this launch. We've hired for the new task, we've allocated this amount of money to get started, we've rearranged priorities, and we've written new job descriptions. We're ready!"

If you plan to launch a new product, explain the results of your market testing. If you want to build a new building,

> The stakeholders intuitively ask, "Can you really do this? Are you ready?"

tell them how you've met with the city zoning board to get the necessary permits. Talk about how you've rearranged your structure so the new organizational chart reflects the additional responsibilities. Through all your explanations, paint a clear picture of how all these efforts will meet a pressing need and change lives. A compelling vision touches hearts, and a clear plan inspires minds and soothes fears.

When you are exposed to another leader's grand idea, stop and ask, "What need is it meeting?" Opening a new store may make sense, but only if it puts your company in an area where your products aren't readily available. Building a larger church building doesn't make sense if you're not reaching a new demographic group and your current facilities aren't bursting at the seams. A new program for young couples doesn't make sense unless you want to attract couples who have pressing needs to learn how to be good spouses, loving parents, and skilled in managing their money. Today convenience is a high value, so a church may meet this need by providing easy access to services, or a pharmacy may offer to mail prescriptions instead of having people come to the store.

Look more deeply to discover the real needs in people's lives. They don't need a new building, program, or product, but the building, program, or product may be an effective way to meet their need.

When Panama took over at the Canal Zone, needs for the shipping industry were going unmet. The objective to widen the canal wasn't merely to have something bigger and better, but to meet the pressing need to facilitate worldwide shipping. The momentum to expand the locks and dig deeper approaches also came from the possibility of competition. Planners had resurrected the old plans to build a canal across Nicaragua, which might have made the one in Panama obsolete. The Panama Canal Authority then had two pressing needs that propelled them forward: one internal and one external.

As companies found other means to transport goods, causing business at the canal to begin to slip away, the officials at

> Look more deeply to discover the real needs in people's lives.

the authority began to ask, "Why not us? Why not here? Why not now?" They determined that the answer to those questions was clear: there was no better route for shipping, no better systems than the locks, and no better plan than to expand the existing locks to accommodate larger ships. They decided the time was right for a major expansion project.

Go to conferences and listen to the great things other leaders are doing, talk to your friends who are doing wonderful things in their organizations, and read articles and books about bold initiatives, but *don't jump to conclusions*. Stop to reflect on the needs those organizations are meeting. If the same needs exist in your world, consider meeting them, but come up with your own plan to fit your community and circumstances. The reflection, though, may surface a very different need for your organization to meet, or you may realize you're in a consolidation phase to solidify the gains you recently made. But don't wait too long during consolidation: you're moving toward Point B one way or another!

Think, talk to wise people, and stay focused on the pressing needs in your community. If you're not meeting a real need, your plans will generate little initial enthusiasm and even less momentum to sustain the effort. A vision that captures hearts propels the organization forward. With it, you lead motivated people; without it, you drive people and demand compliance. When the vision isn't based on a need, leaders must continually sell people—especially their staff teams—to keep them pumped up, but sooner or later, trust erodes and the team becomes resistant.

When a leadership team is galvanized by the prospect of meeting needs in the lives of people in the community, team members daydream about new ideas almost as much as the leader does. They dive into their work with infectious enthusiasm, sharing their hearts with everyone they meet and creatively overcoming challenges. They do research because they want their efforts to be successful, and they gladly enlist others to join them in the work.

> A vision that captures hearts propels the organization forward.

For instance, a leader may identify the need

to reach out to young adults who feel overlooked in the community. The leader may ask someone on his staff to form a small team of two young couples and three young singles to read about this demographic group, interview many of them, and make a report in a month. Their report to the staff team is based on academic research as well as anecdotal evidence to identify the top five needs in the lives of young adults who live in reasonable proximity to the church.

When the needs are clearly known, then the temporary team or the staff team can begin to craft plans to meet those needs, including programs, facilities, a budget, and—of course—leadership of this effort. When the plans are in place, the church can announce them on communication platforms that connect with this audience. The branding, messaging, and leadership are all shaped by the clear conception of the need they are trying to meet.

RELAUNCH

If you're shrewd enough to anticipate the need for change at Point A on the curve, or if you realize your established business or church is eroding toward Point B, it's time to relaunch your enterprise. Let me make a few suggestions as you consider your next steps.

- *Be ruthlessly honest.* No rose-colored glasses, no blind optimism, and no excuses. Recognize the trajectory of your growth, stagnation, or decline, and have the guts to tell your team and board the unvarnished truth.
- *Take time to dream.* You're only stuck in a rut if you choose to stay there. You can get up and get going again, but you need a North Star, a driving motivation, a dream to capture your imagination. You can't manufacture a

> The branding, messaging, and leadership are all shaped by the clear conception of the need they are trying to meet.

vision. As we've seen, it should come out of a deep sense of needs in the lives of others. If this need isn't met, their lives will be harmed or lacking in a significant way. A dream may crystallize in a moment, but far more often, it takes shape over time. Ask God to give you something that keeps you up at night—not with worry, but with anticipation of what he might do in and through you.

- *Find a good coach or mentor.* We're better when we have a partner, someone who will tell us the truth no matter what that truth may be. We need someone who knows well enough to point out our strengths so we work from them, and who is honest about the yellow and red flags they see in our lives. We need more than a friend; we need a thoroughly objective, insightful person who has been where we want to go and knows how to help us get there.

- *Be a continual learner.* Great leaders are sponges who soak up information. Read challenging books, listen to brilliant speakers on podcasts, and talk to leaders in other fields to see how their expertise might cross-pollinate you and your organization.

- *Trust your instincts.* Most leaders have risen to their positions because they have a sixth sense about people, systems, and opportunities for the future. We've all been burned when our instincts led us to decisions that didn't pan out very well. That's going to happen. But the best leaders don't abandon the gift that got them where they are today. If your instincts are prompting you to lead in a direction that may not be popular, be sure to get input from your coach to confirm your direction and be prepared for resistance.

- *Expect difficulties, but try to avoid creating them.* Leaders have targets in their minds, but they have targets on their backs too. Every significant endeavor is filled with drama, setbacks, and unforeseen circumstances. Don't be shocked when you encounter them, no matter how clearly you believe God is leading you. No one was more in tune with God than Jesus, and his obedience led him to abandonment, ridicule, suffering, and death. Thankfully, very few of us face that kind of difficulty as we follow God, but Jesus invited us to take up our crosses and follow him, so obedience to his call inevitably involves some measure of heartache.

- *Don't opt for the cheapest path.* The Panama Canal Authority picked the consortium that submitted the lowest bid, but cost overruns raised the price higher than the other bids. It's tempting to try to cut corners at the beginning. Get input from experts to be sure your plans and costs are reasonable.

- *Beware of add-on growth.* I've seen farmhouses that added rooms over the years when more children were born, young couples came back to live at home, or grandparents needed care during their last years. These houses began with a workable floor plan, but the additional rooms were added in odd places. After a while, the house looked like a curiosity, with halls and rooms in strange places.

When we plan for growth in our organizations, we need to be careful we're not creating a monstrosity of add-ons. Sometimes, it's best to step back, realize we need a completely new plan, tear down, and rebuild. It costs more at the time of construction, but it will be far more serviceable in the coming years. The metaphor is of a building, but the concept applies to programs, product lines, and markets.

- *Don't lose touch with people.* In the stress and busyness of relaunching an organization, leaders can become preoccupied with details and deadlines and miss the people around them. Take time to talk to your staff about how they're doing, how they're handling their own stress, and how you can help them. And carve out time on a regular basis to spend with the people whose needs the relaunch is trying to meet. Get to know them, listen to their stories, and let their needs touch you again and again.

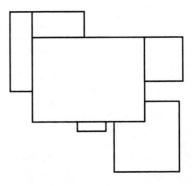

- *Look for the best in every person.* Major transitions in organizations create friction, and friction can easily turn into the smoldering fire of resentment. Make a point of being positive, optimistic, and thankful. When you encounter resistance, be careful not to label those people as "the enemy." Instead, look for strengths in them you can praise and service you can thank them for. Remember: love covers a multitude of sins.

- *Pour yourself into your best people.* It's tempting to devote our time and energy to the few people who are relatively resistant, slow, and ineffective. When we focus on them, we become exhausted and discouraged. Instead, spend more of your energies interacting with your best people, supporting them, and providing resources they need to do an outstanding job. Whenever possible, let someone else handle the others, and when necessary, reassign them or release and replace them.

- *Inspire your team with meaning.* Don't let every meeting sink into the drudgery of detailed reports and boring numbers. Certainly, you should cover important items that relate to systems and structures, but be sure to regularly and passionately make the clear connection to the need and the vision so the tasks will make sense to each person on the team.

- *Keep your own fires burning.* Keep an eye on your joy meter, and make sure it stays on high! Find ways to enjoy your work. All of us have certain parts of our jobs we love and parts we endure. Be sure to spend more time on what you love and less on the rest. This may seem selfish, but it's not. Your team and your vision need you to be enthusiastic and optimistic. In fact, everything depends on your attitude throughout the process.

If this is your last initiative, your last year as the leader in your organization, leave wisely and gracefully. Make succession a pleasant and positive experience for everybody. Don't let factions form. They cripple the new leader and poison the organization. Work with the transition team to select the best person to replace you, make the path smooth for that person by clearly transferring responsibility and loyalty, show people you trust the selection process and the new leader, and then let go when the time comes. Thank God for all he has done through you, and celebrate what God will do in the future.

The Panama Canal was the largest, most challenging building project the world had ever known. Theodore Roosevelt recognized the pressing need for commerce to travel more easily between the oceans, and despite past failures, he believed it was still possible to dig a path in the jungle between the seas. The size and speed of the project required elaborate and expensive systems to carve a mountain down to size, dredge channels on both ports, dam an unpredictable river, and build enormous locks and gates. These systems could only be created by the finest engineers, the most dedicated workers, and the insight of one brilliant doctor. The French spent millions and the lives of twenty-two thousand people in their failed attempt. The American effort took ten long, hard years and cost more than five thousand lives, but when the canal was completed, it magnificently accomplished its purpose.

At the end of his monumental written history of the construction of the canal, David McCullough reflected:

> The creation of a water passage across Panama was one of the supreme human achievements of all time, the culmination of a heroic dream of four hundred years and of more than twenty years of phenomenal effort and sacrifice. The fifty miles between the oceans were among the hardest ever won by human effort and ingenuity, and no statistics on tonnage or tolls can begin to convey the grandeur of what was accomplished. Primarily, the canal is an expression of that old and noble desire to bridge the divide, to bring people together. It is a work of civilization.[1]

Our work as leaders is infused with the same nobility, vision, and difficulty. In our organizations, our task is to bridge the divide between what is and what might be, to bring meaning to those who have lost hope, to bring

> Our task is to bridge the divide between what is and what might be.

value to people who want a better life, and to make human connections richer and more meaningful. Our work as leaders is no less than this, and our challenge is much like the one faced by those who looked at the jungles of Panama and wondered, "Can we really do this?" They answered, "Yes, we can."

That's our answer too.

THINK ABOUT THIS

Reflect on these questions and discuss them with your team:

1. What is your next mountain to climb?
2. Answer these questions:
   - Is the new idea a fine-tuning of the current plan, or is it a drastic leap?
   - Can you accomplish the same objective by going slowly, or can the goal only be fulfilled by being bold? In other words, is the timeline the only real variable?
   - Who is the best person who will listen carefully and give you wise feedback?
   - How will this person help you gather your scattered and conflicting thoughts so they become more cogent?
   - What is the real objective? What will this new idea achieve? What need will it meet?
   - Do you have enough gas in the tank to see the plan to completion? Do you have enough bandwidth to pour time and energy into this project? If not, is there someone who can pick up the baton and carry it across the finish line?
   - Do you have enough emotional margin to handle the resistance

and ridicule? Do you have enough emotional strength to deal with your own self-doubts and second-guessing?

- Will the primary stakeholders get behind this effort?
- All major efforts come at a cost. What will it cost you? What will you have to give up to make this happen?
- Do you need to cast the new vision to create enthusiasm for building the new systems and structures to complete it, or do you need to carefully craft the systems and structures first before you announce the new initiative?

3. Review the suggestions in the last section of the chapter. Which of these do you need to implement soon? What difference will they make?

4. What are the three or four most important principles you've learned from this book? How will you apply them?

Remember: The size and speed of an organization are controlled by its systems and structures.

NOTES

Introduction

1. MI News Network, "AAPA: U.S. Ports Plan to Invest $154 Billion By 2020," Marine Insight, updated April 7, 2016, http://www.marineinsight.com/shipping-news/aapa-u-s-ports-plan-invest-154-billion-2020/.

2. Jim Collins, *Good to Great: Why Some Companies Make the Leap . . . and Others Don't* (New York: HarperCollins, 2001), 13.

Chapter 1: How Do You Define the Need?

1. For more on these phases, look at chapter 7 of my book *Cracking Your Church's Culture Code* (San Francisco: Jossey-Bass, 2011).

2. For much more on organizational culture, look at my book *Cracking Your Church's Culture Code.*

Chapter 2: How Do You Handle Colossal Failure?

1. Max De Pree, *Leadership Is an Art* (New York: Doubleday, 1987), 11.

Chapter 3: Where Do You Find Fresh Passion and Purpose?

1. William Andrews, "The Early Years: The Challenge of Public Order—1845 to 1870," New York City Police Department History Site

at the Wayback Machine, https://web.archive.org/web/20060930063300 /http://nyc.gov/html/nypd/html/3100/retro.html.

2. Peggy Samuels and Harold Samuels, *Teddy Roosevelt at San Juan: The Making of a President* (College Station, TX: Texas A&M University Press, 1997), 266.

3. "Theodore Roosevelt," Miller Center of Public Affairs, University of Virginia, http://millercenter.org/president/roosevelt.

4. Theodore Roosevelt, "First Annual Message" to Congress, December 3, 1901, *The American Presidency Project*, http://www.presidency. ucsb.edu/ws/?pid=29542.

5. Charles Handy, *The Age of Paradox* (Cambridge: Harvard Business Press, 1995), 49–68.

6. For more on the Sigmoid Curve, see my book *Cracking Your Church's Culture Code*, 120–27.

7. John Dewey, *How We Think* (New York: D. C. Heath, 1910), 78, cited by Colin M. Beard and John Peter Wilson, *Experiential Learning: A Handbook for Education, Training, and Coaching*, 3rd ed. (London: Kogan Page, 2013).

8. Brené Brown, *Daring Greatly: How the Courage to Be Vulnerable Transforms the Way We Live, Love, Parent and Lead* (New York: Penguin Books, 2012), 37.

9. "Then and Now: The Panama Canal," American Experience, PBS, http://www.pbs.org/wgbh/americanexperience/features/then-and -now/panama/.

Chapter 4: How Do You Craft the Right Plan?

1. Stevens's observations to Shonts, December 19, 1905, in David McCullough, *The Path Between the Seas: The Creation of the Panama Canal, 1870–1914* (New York: Simon & Schuster, 1977), 480.

2. Ibid., 481.

3. From Murrow's testimony as the director of USIA before a Congressional Committee, May 1963. "About U.S. Public Diplomacy," PublicDiplomacy.org, http://pdaa.publicdiplomacy.org/?page_id=6.

4. Dwight D. Eisenhower, "The President's News Conference," November 14, 1956, The American Presidency Project, http://www .presidency.ucsb.edu/ws/?pid=10702.

Chapter 5: What's in Your Suitcase?

1. William Manchester, *A World Lit Only by Fire: The Medieval Mind and the Renaissance* (New York: Little, Brown, 1992), 22.

2. Richard A. Swenson, *Margin: Restoring Emotional, Physical, Financial, and Time Reserves to Overloaded Lives* (Colorado Springs: NavPress, 2004), 60.

3. Robert P. Jones, "The Eclipse of White Christian America," *Atlantic*, July 12, 2016, http://www.theatlantic.com/politics/archive/2016/07 /the-eclipse-of-white-christian-america/490724/.

4. David McCullough, *The Path Between the Seas: The Creation of the Panama Canal, 1870–1914* (New York: Simon & Schuster, 1977), 438.

Chapter 6: You Didn't Expect This, Did You?

1. Comment by Dr. Alexander Lambert, cited in "Yellow Fever and Malaria in the Canal," American Experience, PBS, http://www.pbs .org/wgbh/americanexperience/features/general-article/panama-fever/.

2. See Genesis 3; 27; 29:14–30:21; Numbers 11.

Chapter 7: How Do You Handle Opposition?

1. David McCullough, *The Path Between the Seas: The Creation of the Panama Canal, 1870–1914* (New York: Simon & Schuster, 1977), 503–4.

2. Stevens letter of January 30, 1907, I.C.C records, *Annual Reports 1904–1914.*

3. "N. T. Wright Quotes—Page 3," AZ Quotes, http://www.azquotes. com/author/15971-N_T_Wright?p=3.

Chapter 8: How Can You Make Your Systems Hum?

1. Joseph Bucklin Bishop and Farnham Bishop, *Goethals: Genius of the Panama Canal; A Biography* (New York: Harper and Bros., 1930), 144.

2. Brian Herbert and Kevin J. Anderson, *Dune: House Harkonnen* (New York: Bantam Books, 2000), 532.

Chapter 10: How Can You Produce Creative Tension?

1. Walter Leon Pepperman, *Who Built the Panama Canal?* (New York: E. P. Dutton, 1915), 125.

2. David McCullough, *The Path Between the Seas: The Creation of the Panama Canal, 1870–1914* (New York: Simon & Schuster, 1977), 504.

3. Peter Drucker, *Management: Tasks, Responsibilities, Practices* (New York: Routledge, 2011), 379.

Chapter 11: Does It Ever End?

1. Adapted from Rick Warren's concepts outlined in *The Purpose Driven Church* (Grand Rapids: Zondervan, 1995), and more specifically in Make Believe, *Purpose Driven Campaigning: 40 Key Principles for Growing Social Movements* (Surrey, AU: Make Believe), http://www.jrmyprtr.com/wordpress/wp-content/uploads/2014/01/purpose-driven-campaigning.pdf.

2. See Matthew 14:13–21; Mark 6:30–44; Luke 9:10–17; John 6:1–15.

3. Vanderbloemen Search Group and the Unstuck Group, *Next Level Teams: How Fast-Growing Churches Are Mobilizing Their Staff*, 13, available at https://tonymorganlive.com/store/next-level-teams/.

Chapter 12: What's the Next Big Dream?

1. David McCullough, *The Path Between the Seas: The Creation of the Panama Canal, 1870–1914* (New York: Simon & Schuster, 1977), 613–14.

BIBLIOGRAPHY

Much of the information about the building of the Panama Canal comes from David McCullough's *The Path Between the Seas* (New York: Simon & Schuster, 1977).

Other sources include the following:

American Experience. "Then & Now: The Panama Canal." PBS. http://www.pbs .org/wgbh/americanexperience/features/then-and-now/panama/.

———. "Theodore Roosevelt and the Panama Canal." PBS. http://www.pbs.org /wgbh/americanexperience/features/general-article/tr-panama/.

———. "Timeline: Creating the Canal." PBS. http://www.pbs.org/wgbh /americanexperience/features/timeline/panama/.

———. "Yellow Fever and Malaria in the Canal." PBS. http://www.pbs.org/wgbh /americanexperience/features/general-article/panama-fever.

Bishop, Joseph Bucklin. *Goethals: Genius of the Panama Canal; A Biography.* New York: Harper and Bros., 1930.

Bogdanich, Walt, Ana Graciela Mendez, and Jacqueline Williams. "Panama Takes $3 Billion Bet on Wider Canal." *International New York Times,* June 24, 2016.

Brown, Brené. *Daring Greatly.* New York: Penguin Books, 2012.

Bryant, Adam. "When Titles Get in the Way." *New York Times,* Business, June 6, 2014.

Caraballo, Hector. "Emergency Department Management of Mosquito-Borne Illness: Malaria, Dengue, and West Nile Virus." *Emergency Medicine Practice,* May 2014.

"Central American Canal Routes Considered." *The Geography of Transport Systems.* https://people.hofstra.edu/geotrans/eng/ch1en/appl1en/map _central_american_canal_routes.html.

Collins, Jim. *Good to Great.* New York: HarperCollins, 2001.

De Pree, Max. *Leadership Is an Art.* New York: Doubleday, 1987.

Drucker, Peter. *Management.* New York: Taylor & Francis Group, 1974.

Fierman, William. "The New Panama Canal Is Opening Soon and Will Cause an 'Evolution' in a Vital US Industry." *Business Insider,* May 2016.

"HMS *Dreadnought* Dreadnought Battleship." Military Factory. http://www .militaryfactory.com/ships/detail.asp?ship_id=HMS-Dreadnought.

Isthmian Canal Commission. *Annual Reports 1904–1914.*

Jackson, Eric. "8 Reasons Your Best People Are About to Quit—and How You Can Keep Them." *Forbes,* May 11, 2014.

Jones, Robert P. "The Eclipse of White Christian America." *Atlantic,* July 12, 2016. http://www.theatlantic.com/politics/archive/2016/07/the-eclipse-of -white-christian-america/490724/.

Kotter, John P. "Leading Change: Why Transformation Efforts Fail." *Harvard Business Review,* March–April 1995.

Lapin, David. "How Intangible Corporate Culture Creates Tangible Profits." *Fast Company,* June 20, 2012. https://www.fastcompany.com/1840650/how -intangible-corporate-culture-creates-tangible-profits.

Manchester, William. *A World Lit Only by Fire.* New York: Little, Brown, 1992.

McCullough, David. *Mornings on Horseback: The Story of an Extraordinary Family, a Vanished Way of Life, and the Unique Child Who Became Theodore Roosevelt.* New York: Simon & Schuster, 1981.

Morgan, Tony, and William Vanderbloemen. *Next Level Teams: How Fast- Growing Churches Are Mobilizing Their Staff.* Available at https:// tonymorganlive.com/store/next-level-teams/.

Panama Canal Authority. "The French Canal Construction." PanCanal.com. http://www.pancanal.com/eng/history/history/french.html.

Panama Canal History. "Design of the Locks." PanCanal.com. http://www .pancanal.com/eng/history/history/locks.html.

Panama Canal Railway. "Construction of the First Transcontinental Railroad." Panarail.com. http://panarail.com/en/history/index.html.

Paris, Costas, Robbie Whelan, and Kejal Vyas. "The Panama Canal Expands." *Wall Street Journal,* June 20, 2016.

Pepperman, Walter Leon. *Who Built the Panama Canal?* New York: E. P. Dutton, 1915.

Phillips-Birt, Douglas. "How Big Can Ships Grow?" *New Scientist*, December 31, 1970.

Roosevelt, Theodore. "First Annual Message" to Congress. December 3, 1901. *The American Presidency Project*. http://www.presidency.ucsb.edu/ws/?pid =29542.

Solem, Borge. "The Giant Express Steamers." Norway Heritage. http://www .norwayheritage.com/express-steamers.htm.

Swenson, Richard. *Margin*. Colorado Springs: Navpress, 2004.

Wile, Rob. "100 Years After Its Birth, the Panama Canal Is on the Verge of Creating a Huge New Opportunity for US Exporters." *Business Insider*, August 17, 2014. http://www.businessinsider.com/panama-canal-expansion -redefine-trade-2014–8.

ABOUT DR. SAM CHAND

Who would have thought, when in 1973 "student" Dr. Sam Chand was serving Beulah Heights Bible College as janitor, cook and dishwasher, that he would return in 1989 as "President" of the same college! Under his leadership it became the country's largest predominantly African-American Bible College.

Dr. Sam Chand is a former Pastor, college President, Chancellor and now serves as President Emeritus of Beulah Heights University.

In this season of his life, Dr. Sam Chand does one thing--Leadership. His singular vision for his life is Helping Others Succeed.

Dr. Sam Chand Develops Leaders Through:

- Leadership Consultations
- Leadership Resources--Books, CDs, DVDs
- Leadership Speaking
- Dream Releaser Coaching
- Dream Releaser Publishing

As a Dream Releaser he serves Pastors, ministries and businesses as a Leadership Architect and Change Strategist. Dr. Sam Chand speaks regularly at leadership conferences, churches, corporations, ministerial conferences, seminars and other leadership development opportunities.

Dr. Sam Chand...

- Consults with large churches and businesses on leadership and capacity enhancing issues
- Named in the top-30 global Leadership Gurus list
- Founder & President of Dream Releaser Coaching and Dream Releaser Publishing
- Conducts nationwide Leadership Conferences
- Serves on the board of Beulah Heights University
- Serves on the board of Advisors of EQUIP (Dr. John Maxwell's ministry), equipping 5 million leaders world-wide

www.samchand.com

CONSULTATION

"IT'S NEVER TOO LATE TO BE WHAT YOU MIGHT HAVE BEEN."
- GEORGE ELIOT

Are you at the intersection of
"Where you want to be?" and **"Where you want to go?"**

YOU NEED A DREAM RELEASER

A DREAM RELEASER is what I was built to be.

DISCOVERIES AS A DREAM RELEASER:

- After a certain level, you are finding fewer people who can understand you and your needs.
- After a certain level, you are finding it difficult to identify credible, and trusted counsel.
- After a certain level, your own dreams scare you!

I will be your DREAM RELEASER by serving you in two primary roles:

1. LEADERSHIP ARCHITECT

This is where I hear your dream, understand your vision and context and provide you with a customized blueprint to release your dreams.

2. CHANGE STRATEGIST

All dream releasing entails different levels and consequences of change. I provide you with a detailed step-by-step change strategy.

So, what do I BRING to you?

As A DREAM RELEASER I Develop Leaders Who Reproduce More Leaders

DEVELOPING: Training focuses on the task and is single-focused, whereas development focuses on the person and is multi-dimensional.

LEADERS: People who can see it (KNOW) pursue it on their own (GROW) and help others see it (SHOW).

REPRODUCING MORE LEADERS: A leadership culture with an action bias that makes leadership reproduction a natural process.

www.samchand.com

  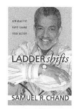  

  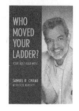